MW01232132

Silence

It's not the shouting
Or the angry words
It's not those looks
Sideways Glancing
It's not do as I say
It's not compliance

It's the silence
It's the silence

It's not the reasoning
It's not the logic
It's not the questions
Third degrees
It's not acceptance
No, it's not defiance

It's the silence
It's the silence

Fear of the unknown
Is bad enough, yeah
But saying nothing
Says so much

It's the silence
It's the silence
It's the silence
(Yeah)
It's the silence
No more silence
No more silence
No more silence
No more silence
Wait a minute, no more silence
Stand up better, shout it out, shout it out
Silence, yeah
Won't you please shout it out, silence?

No more, no more silence
No, no, no, no, no, no, no
No more silence, please, please, please
No more silence, no more silence, yeah

Scream a minute, scream a minute
Silence, yeah, yeah, stop it now, stop it now
Silence, please, no more, please no more
Please, no more, please no more silence
Oh, no, no, no, no more silence
Please, no more silence

No, no, no, no, no, no, no
No more silence, please, please, please
No more silence, no more silence, yeah

Scream a minute, scream a minute
Silence, yeah, yeah, stop it now stop it now
Silence, please no more, please no more
Please no more, please no more silence
No, no, no, no, no more silence
Please, no more silence

Lyrics by Corey Glover

The Silent Integrators: Transitioning from Segregation to Integration

(L-R) Lonnie J. Edwards and Hansell Gunn, Jr.

The
Lonnie J. Edwards, Sr., Ed. D.
and
Hansell Gunn, Jr., Ed. S.
Story

ISBN: 979-8-9854411-2-3

Mother to Son
By LANGSTON HUGHES

Well, son, I'll tell you:

Life for me ain't been no crystal stair.

It's had tacks in it,

And splinters,

And boards torn up,

And places with no carpet on the floor—

Bare.

But all the time

I've been a-climb in' on,

And reachin' landin's,

And turnin' corners,

And sometimes goin' in the dark

Where there ain't been no light.

So boy, don't you turn back.

Don't you set down on the steps

'Cause you finds it's kinder hard.

'Don't you fall now—

For I'se still going', honey,

I'se still climbing',

And life for me ain't been no crystal stair.

TABLE OF CONTENTS

PROLOGUE

Transitioning from Segregation to Integration
- *A unique journey in human relations - from Mississippi, Alabama, Georgia, and the Southeastern United States.*

There were Federal Government assessments, but no one marching... no one standing in doors, blocking entrances ... no city or community disturbances ... no military or secret service escorts or police supervision ... no student walkouts in protest ... and no one was killed.

It all happened in Montevallo, Alabama ...

- 30 miles from Birmingham, Alabama
  - (where a bomb [the third in 11 days] made of 15 sticks of dynamite, planted by members of the Ku Klux Klan – resisting integration, exploded during Sunday morning services in the 16th Street Baptist Church, killing four young girls: Addie Mae Collins (14), Cynthia Wesley (14), Carole Robertson (14) and Carol Denise McNair (11).)

- 50 miles from Selma, Alabama
  - (best known for the activism of the1960's civil rights movement and "Bloody Sunday," the voting rights march over the Edmund Pettus Bridge).

- 55 miles from the University of Alabama in Tuscaloosa, Alabama
  - (where Governor George Wallace blocked Vivien Malone and James Hood from entering the university and sent more than one hundred state troopers to stop the federal court-ordered integration of public schools) ...

- 60 miles from Montgomery, Alabama
  - (where Governor Wallace closed public schools, state-wide, rather than integrate; where the community organized the Montgomery Transportation Boycotts) ...

- 134 miles from Philadelphia, MS
  - (where buried in an earthen dam, three civil rights workers were found. Michael Schwerner and Andrew Goodman, both white New Yorkers, had traveled to heavily segregated Mississippi in 1964 to help organize civil rights efforts on behalf of the Congress of Racial Equality (CORE). The third man, James Chaney, was a local African American man who had joined CORE in 1963. The disappearance of the three young men led to a massive FBI investigation that was code-named MIBURN, for "Mississippi Burning") ...
- 175 miles from Oxford, MS and the civil unrest at Ole Miss [the University of Mississippi]
  - (where a riot to block James Meredith from attending killed two and injured more than 300 people) ...

- 200 miles from Jackson, MS
  - (where civil rights leader Medgar Evers was slain in the driveway of his own home) ...

- 245 miles from the University of Georgia in Athens, GA
  - (where state legislators passed legislation mandating an immediate cut-off of state funds to any white institution that admitted a black student; where federal district court Judge W. A. Bootle ordered the immediate admission of Hamilton Holmes and Charlayne Hunter, ending 160 years of segregation at the school; and where an angry mob gathered outside Hunter's dormitory, causing significant property damage and garnering negative publicity for the university and the state.)

The small, busy town of Montevallo, Alabama and the University of Montevallo (formerly Alabama College) made integration happen without national attention. It was not without challenges, but it happened peacefully. What a victory!

Often change comes at you with a loud bang, creating a stir; sometimes it evolves ever so quietly, like a butterfly floating in the air effortlessly. Sometimes noise interrupts that peace, shattering the still quietness. However, silence can blend into the setting, inconspicuous and subtle, changing the landscape with an unassuming and unexpected influence.

DEDICATION
From the Author, Alvin P. Edwards

Frances Alberta Johnson Burton, my mom, my friend, my confidante, my rock. My mother's parenting skills helped my siblings and me to always feel valued and to know that we deserved to be treated with dignity and respect. Her teachings made us strong and self-confident. I am grateful to have had her actively engaged in my life and sincerely appreciate her encouraging me to pursue my dream of becoming a writer.

Billy Edwards, my brother who taught me how to fight, persevere, and stay positive.

Alfred Edwards, my brother who fueled my competitive spirit and kept me striving.

Ray Edwards, my brother who showed and taught me how to be compassionate and instilled in me a love of sports.

Beverly Burton, my only sister, my friend, and confidante who has been my most avid supporter. I have been inspired by just watching her grow up and become an awesome woman.

Karen Edwards, my wife, for her loving support and patience with me during my late night and early morning writing binges.

Hansell Gunn, Jr., my new big brother who I never knew until I took this journey with him, and he shared his story with me. He is an inspiration not only to me, but to his siblings and others who know him, leading with courage and fortitude.

Dr. Lonnie Johnson Edwards, Sr., my brother who I follow in age by ten years. As I was growing up, I could never keep up with him because he was always coming in and going out, leaving only shadows. But this journey has helped me to understand why he was darting as he did. By sharing the details of his life, now as adults, he's allowed me to catch up. During our daily chats, I have learned so much more about him and his life's journey. So, for fun, I began posting some of the highlights on Facebook. As time went on, and Facebook readers were hungry for more, I was inspired to move from online Facebook to a hard copy book. Listening to the many challenges, obstacles, and humiliating situations that Lonnie and Hansell endured, as well as of their courage, boldness, and victories, along with their impacts on so many lives, kindled a desire in me to share their stories with the world. The parallel lives of the two can encourage others to never give in to adversity and serve as a motivator to live a life of purpose.

Thank you, my brothers!

ACKNOWLEDGEMENTS

From the Author, Alvin P. Edwards

Special "Thanks" are extended to:

A host of local newspapers, high school and college yearbooks, Readers' Digest, and sources of organizational awards documenting Lonnie's and Hansell's journeys.

Facebook, for providing a forum to introduce excerpts of this story to an audience and to gain feedback and interest in more.

Nancy Johnson Miller, Lonnie's former fifth grade student, for her public expression of gratitude on the Sally Jessy Raphael Show, acknowledging his making a difference in her life and for granting me an interview for this book.

Sources providing pictures and documentation to support the historical authenticity of this book:
- Wilda Gunn
- Herbert Gunn
- Coahoma Community College
- The University of Montevallo

Cynthia Dorsey Edwards, my sister-in-law, for her reading, editing, and guidance in preparing this book for printing and publication.

ACKNOWLEDGEMENTS

Dr. Lonnie J. Edwards, Sr.

Considering all, my first honor and thanks is to God for his ever presence, guidance, and direction in my life. I thank Him for blessing me with my talents and skills and acknowledge that my accomplishments could not have been achieved without Him. I have lived by faith with God's mercy and grace. My guiding Bible verse is Philippians 4:13 which says, "I can do all things through Christ who strengthens me."

God has truly blessed me to be a husband to the late Brenda Dobbs Edwards, and presently to Cynthia Dorsey Edwards; father to Ulric, Lonnie Jr., and Lynda; Father-in- law to Ebony, Susan, and Aaron; and Grandfather to Lanee', Lia, Jada, Jaden, Lonnie III, and Ariana.

Reflecting on my life, I think of all of the people who have contributed to my personal development and professional success. While there are too many to mention by name, I hope that everyone reading this book will remember our encounters positively and know that I have appreciated each of you whether you were in my life for "a reason, a season, or a lifetime."

That said, there are a few people for whom I am compelled to give special recognition and express appreciation for their influences in my life:

My Maternal Grandparents: Louis and Abbie Johnson
I have a vivid memory of my grandmother! My words cannot adequately express the strong feelings I have when I think of my amazing grandmother, affectionately called "Ms. Pat" by everyone who knew her. Although she had a fifth-grade education, she and my grandfather, who also had a limited formal education, bought a hundred acres of land. She taught me about God, how to pray and love life, to care for others, and to always give to help others in need. She not only taught me how to work the farm, but also how to read and make

speeches, and so much more. Most of all, my grandmother taught me that no matter how challenging the circumstances, to "never, ever give up."

---Forever grateful---

My Father and Mother: Lonnie Lee and Frances Johnson Edwards

Sharecroppers and landowners; strong-willed and focused. Their marriage lasted for seven years, during which I, and thirteenth months later, my brother Billy, was born. My father and mother divorced. Both remarried and carried on their separate lives.

--- Loved them both! ---

My Brothers and Special Sister:

Billy, Sammie, Sanders, Charles, Ollie, Alfred, Ray, Alvin, Darrell, and Beverly

To be an example is a challenging assignment filled with trials and errors. I cannot recall the number of times that I've failed and/or missed the goal, but neither quitting nor giving up was an option. YOU WERE WATCHING! Throughout my journey, you were on my mind. You inspired me to keep going!

--- Keep the faith! ---

My Mother's Siblings:

Sisters - Minnie, Annette, Ruby, and Bertha; brothers - Louis and James (J P) Collins (adopted). They all surrounded me with love and encouragement and contributed to teaching me about farm life: driving the tractors, feeding the livestock, and picking cotton. Bertha took the role of Lil' Mama and married a wonderful man, James (Big Cuz) Rodges, who embraced the roles and served as my father image, advisor, and counselor until his death in 2018.

--- Priceless and thankful ---

My High School and College Coaches, Teammates, Teachers, and Community Leaders who helped to shape my character and nurtured my drive, especially:
- Coach James Rodges; Coach Herman Smith, Physical Education; Ms. Easter Sharp, English; Ms. Evelyn Byrd, English; Billy Joe McCain, Business Education, community leader and my mentor
- Coach William "Pop" Gaines, Head Basketball Coach at Coahoma Junior College, for his wise counsel and encouragement to consider becoming an agent of change in the evolving society.

The Administrators and Staff at Alabama College/University of Montevallo who, in 1969, had the courage to facilitate integration and to foster the acceptance of differences:
- Kermit A. Johnson, President
- Dr. Leon Davis, Athletic Director
- Coach Bill Jones, Men's Head Basketball Coach
- B.E. Fancher, Dean of Education
- Kermit Mathis, Director of Admissions and Records
- Dr. James R. Wilkinson, Dean of Men and Family
- W. F. Wallace, Psychology Professor
- Dr. Jeanette Crew, Professor (taught square dancing)
- Linda J. Hammett, Professor (taught Hansell and me to swim)
- Thomas M. Fleming, Assistant Professor
- Drs. Frank and Bobbye Lightfoot, Professors (my Montevallo parents)
- Many others

The University of Montevallo Men's Basketball Team of 1969-1971:
Special appreciation to James Hobbs who always encouraged Hansell and me and showed extraordinary support to us in so many ways.

Family members – paternal and maternal, classmates, teammates, professional colleagues, mentors, personal friends, faith-based leaders, and contemporaries in the DeKalb County School District, the Georgia Department of Education, and the Jackson Public School System:

Thank you for being on this journey with me, providing encouragement, wise insights, wisdom, support, advice, counsel, and guidance through the dark days and challenging times as well as helping me to celebrate successes. It would have been a more difficult journey without you. Together, we have made a difference!

My unofficial, adopted brother, Earnest Killum
A unique, college teammate and an unofficial, adopted brother. Our relationship lasted for 51 years - through basketball gymnasiums and games, colleges, churches, work settings, and countless social gatherings. His drive and tireless efforts made me better as a basketball player – earning invites to NBA pro camps. I guess I made him better too. He was a second-round draft choice for the Los Angeles Lakers. He gifted me with my first airline ticket. (Of course, it's a story behind it.) We supported each other through studies for college graduations ---Associates, Masters, and Doctoral programs --- although he chose not to complete his doctoral dissertation (ABD). We were road buddies, traveling throughout the United States; the "Best Man" in each other's weddings; and "Uncle" to each other's children. Our friendship evolved into our brotherhood. Thanks, Earnie, for the memories!

> *"There are friends, there is family,*
> *and then there are friends that become family."*
> *- Unknown*

--- In death did we part. ---

My God-given partner, Hansell Gunn, Jr.
Matthew 22:14 NKJV, Jesus says, "For many are called, but few are chosen." At the beginning of our journey as young, black men from the Mississippi Delta, we did not know our similarities and did not understand the path put before us. Now, I know that we were called to be on a divine mission for "human development" --- ours and others. We took the path less traveled. The journey with Hansell was not only dark and risky, but on many occasions, frightening and dangerous. But we weathered the storms, and now, we leave a blueprint for others to follow and to know that such a mission is possible.

--- To God be the glory! ---

My brother, Alvin Patrick Edwards
He listened to stories of my life that he never knew and thought enough of them ... as well as of Hansell and me ... to put pen to paper, sharing them to encourage and inspire others. I value our daily chats as well as his love and enthusiasm. I appreciate all that he has done to bring this book into existence. May this be just the beginning of a new and exciting chapter in his life!

--- So proud! ---

My wife, Cynthia Dorsey Edwards
Proverbs 18:22 NKJV says, *"He who* finds a wife finds a good *thing, And* obtains favor from the LORD." Cynthia is a perfect partner for me and blend for our family. She is blessed with intelligence, insight, passion, compassion, grace, and focus, all which have contributed to our successfully navigating challenges and changes while making progress and impact during a huge part of my/our lives and careers. Much love and appreciation.

--- A Ram in the Bush ---

ACKNOWLEDGEMENTS

Hansell Gunn, Jr., Ed. S.

First of all, I give honor and thanks to God for all the good things He has placed in my life. I thank Him for the challenges too, because it all molded me into the man, husband, and father I am today. Thank you, God, for your many Blessings and the Grace you provide each day of our lives, enabling us to take on the daily tasks.

There were always so many things I wanted to share with the people in my life about my various experiences, the knowledge I gained, and the lessons I learned in my lifetime. I especially wanted to share my time at Montevallo; one of the most confusing, complex and critical periods of my life. The events played out in my mind for years, but I had no idea of how to compile these thoughts or where to begin publishing them. I did not get here by myself; there was so much help along the way. I would like to take the opportunity to say, "Thank You" to some of the wonderful people that helped make my journey possible.

My Mother: Clytee Ballard
Whose strength and toughness kept our family together and pushed us through very difficult circumstances. She provided us with the opportunity to live a better life and acquire a better education. Her example taught us Love of God and family.

My Siblings: Barbara Gunn Jones and Herbert Gunn
Thank you for your love and support! You have always inspired me to "Hang in There," and to "Never give up and never quit!" I am so proud of the man and woman you have become! My sister received a B. S. Degree from Mississippi State University, and my brother received his from the University of Mississippi.

My Grandparents: Willie and Myrtle Townsend and Louise Gunn

My Maternal Grandparents' tough resolve and entrepreneurial sense kept us all on the right track, instilled in us the value of an honest day's work and the pride of home ownership. My Grandmother Louise showed tenderness, love and compassion, the value of family relationships and always having each other's backs.

Teachers

"Thank You" to the teachers who molded and shaped my life in those early years in West Point, Mississippi, particularly Mrs. Pearl Holliway and Mrs. Shirley Williams.

Coaches

"Thank you", Coach William "Pop" Gaines, for your invaluable lessons in team effort, Individual contribution, and commitment. I appreciate the opportunity to play under your tutelage. I learned much!
To Coach Bill Jones and Athletic Director Dr. Leon Davis, "Thank you" for recruiting me and giving me the chance to be an example of patience, capability, and courage to people who thought Lonnie and I were incapable, inept, and admitted to the college by mistake.

Friends

This book would not have been possible without Lonnie Edwards, my "Brother in Arms" and his brother and author, Alvin Edwards. Lonnie and I bonded as friends during the most challenging times in our early twenties. We became brothers!

My Wife, Wilda Vines Gunn; Daughter, Leslie M. Gunn; and Son, Jonathan M. Gunn

My family has been incredibly supportive of my endeavors, making many sacrifices, and, in some cases, offering much encouragement to others. Regardless of what is needed, composing or researching written material, working on fundraisers, contacting public figures or professional sports organizations to establish relationships, or to obtain media attention/support for a project, I can always depend on my family.

FOREWORD

It's the late 1940's. A small town in central Alabama. Montevallo. Home of Alabama College, now the University of Montevallo (UM). A loving mother in rural South Alabama is reluctant about sending her daughter to attend this college. Would she be safe? Would she be accepted? Would she be successful? Who would take care of her? These same feelings were shared by her entire family. She was popular among the students and was chosen as a class favorite. Several faculty members gave her valuable advice to ensure her success. She graduated with a Bachelor of Science Degree in Physical Education and even completed a Master of Science Degree in Education, also at Montevallo. She taught, raised a family, and later earned a Doctorate in Education.

It's the late 1960's. A small town in central Alabama. Montevallo was the home of Alabama College, now the University of Montevallo. A loving Mississippi mother was reluctant about sending her son to attend this college. Would he be safe? Would he be accepted? Would he be successful? Who would take care of him? These same feelings were shared by his entire family. He was popular among the students and was chosen as a class favorite. Several faculty members gave him valuable advice to ensure his success. He graduated with a Bachelor of Science Degree in Physical Education and even completed a Master of Science Degree in Education, also at Montevallo. He taught, raised a family, and later earned a Doctorate in Education.

These two stories read almost identical however, they could not be further apart. The female student is my mother. The male student is my brother, from another mother, Dr. Lonnie Edwards. My mother was Caucasian, and Lonnie is African American. I have heard my parents say many times that when Lonnie came through the gates at Montevallo, no one saw color, they saw a fun-loving new friend, a talented athlete, a serious student, and someone that got along with everyone. It was obvious that Lonnie was raised to respect others and in return he would be respected. And he was. He was treated just like any other student by the faculty and his fellow students. There was no need to accentuate the difference in skin color when you get to know "plain ole Lonnie," as my dad would say. This was at a time when there were only three or four African American students on campus. Integration was in full progress and a hot button across America. Amazingly, Lonnie's positive personality traits masked the difference in his skin color. That is why Montevallo fell in love with him.

My parents, Drs. Frank and Bobbye Lightfoot, both professors at UM, took a liking to this new student and the lifelong relationship began. It was not uncommon for my parents to get close to their students. My brothers and I were very accustomed to students popping in at our home. Some were in tears because their significant other had hurt their feelings, or some stopped by because they just needed a home-cooked meal.

Sometimes, Lonnie brought the only other black student-athlete, at the time, his roommate, Hansell Gunn with him. They were a unique blend – Lonnie, an extrovert and Hansell, an introvert.

I can't remember another student who touched their hearts like Lonnie. We often laugh about a time when Lonnie and Hansell returned to Montevallo for a function. My parents invited them to stay at their home and insisted that Lonnie sleep in my old bedroom.
They were going to meet friends that night, and mother told them that they had a curfew of 11:00 p.m. That's the way she treated her children.

My parents love Lonnie's wife, Cynthia, as much (or maybe more) as they love him. I would drop in to see my parents, and mother would be on the phone with Cynthia.
Those were some long phone calls.

It has been over fifty years now and our relationship could not be any stronger. Mother passed away suddenly in 2019. When our family gathered, Lonnie and Cynthia were right there. Lonnie is a loyal and generous son of the University of Montevallo and of the Lightfoot family also! The Montevallo parallel between my mother and Lonnie was surprising to me. Their similarities greatly outweighed their differences, which is probably what encouraged their bond. This is a beautiful example of when human relations are bonded with respect and love.

I hope that you enjoy this book, **The Silent Integrators**. I am honored to record some memories of Lonnie's arrival into our lives. We know his Montevallo story the best, and there was nothing "silent" about him joining our family! We are proud of Lonnie, Cynthia, and their family as well as of Hansell. We celebrate their accomplishments and the positive examples they set for us all.

Kirk Lightfoot, for the Lightfoot Family

REFLECTIONS FROM A FELLOW STUDENT

The sixties were very turbulent and frightening times for people of color in the deep south. In January 1963, during his inauguration speech, Alabama's governor, George C. Wallace, decreed "segregation today... segregation tomorrow... segregation forever." In June of that same year, Wallace had to be forcefully removed from blocking two (2) black students from enrolling at the University of Alabama. President John F. Kennedy had the National Guard intervene. Five months later, President Kennedy was assassinated.

This was a time of church bombings, KKK rallies, lynchings, and all sorts of unimaginable acts of intimidation to keep Black people "in their place!" In April of 1968, the greatest Black leader ever, Dr. Martin Luther King Jr., was assassinated. Two months later, Robert Kennedy, a presidential hopeful and brother of President John Kennedy was assassinated.

We were scared, our parents were terrified for us to attend "white" schools. In the fall of 1969, the new University of Montevallo (formerly named Alabama College), in an attempt to integrate their basketball team, recruited Lonnie Edwards and Hansell Gunn, Jr. from Coahoma Junior College, an historically, all-black community college in Clarksdale, Mississippi. They were ambassadors for change, and I am sure that they felt the pressure.

Lonnie and Hansell both were great athletes. Lonnie played point guard on the varsity basketball team, while Hansell played forward on the varsity basketball team and in the outfield on the baseball team also. But they weren't just great athletes, they were very good students as well, perfect ambassadors.

I enrolled at the University of Montevallo in the fall semester 1970. Lonnie (Road Dog) Edwards was one of the first persons that I met. He was in the gymnasium greeting the new freshmen, talking trash, full of swagger, always in his "gear" --- basketball shorts, converse sneakers, and pullover, with his gold tooth smiling.

Hansell was just the opposite, quiet and introspective. Lonnie had a name for nearly everyone. My nickname from Lonnie was "Big Apple." He would often tell me that his hardest job was keeping me out of trouble because, no, I wasn't silent.

Hansell Gunn was, truly, the silent integrator. He oft times had to sit on the bench when he knew that he should be playing. Rarely, would the coach of the basketball team play him and Lonnie at the same time. Hansell had the purest, softest jump shot that I had ever seen. He was Steph Curry before Steph was born.

Today, when a jump shooter shoots that high arching jump shot, the commentator proclaims that the shot was wet. Well, Hansell's jumper was damp. You see his jumper didn't come down hard like rain, but instead was more like soft, misty, morning dew on a fall Seattle morning. And that's one of the few times you would hear him talk smack. He would say, " If it hit any net, I don't want it. Give it to the other team!"

Lonnie was a starter and a star on the basketball team. He was a great scorer but was equally respected for his defense. I remember "Road Dog" falling while guarding an opposing player, turning a flip, and coming up still guarding that player. Hansell was the only black player on the baseball team, and you knew when something had happened on the trip to the game. Hansell would internalize his emotions and just stay silent about his experiences with the baseball team for days and days before finally sharing what was bothering him. There were times when he wanted to leave, but he stayed and persevered. And there were times when if Lonnie's and Hansell's parents had known what both of them were going through, they probably would have removed them. Sometimes the silence was deafening!!!

Robert E. Taylor

Chapter 1
The Origins of the Silent Integrators

They can be seen emerging out from under the shadows of isolation, insulation, segregation, and the red Mississippi mud, walking out of their grandparents' cotton fields and off their farms. Two young black boys, a year apart in age, traveling with a sense of purpose and urgency, become change agents, choosing to bridge the gaps between segregated worlds. They are the *Silent Integrators*, coming from rural American towns, Shaw and Egypt, Mississippi.

The Silent Integrators focuses on the lives of both Lonnie Johnson Edwards, Sr. and Hansell Gunn, Jr. before and after picking up basketballs and baseballs, becoming collegiate Hall of Famers, one of them dawning a doctorate robe, and both ascending to the superintendency in different school districts in their home state of Mississippi.

Lonnie is the grandson of the late Abbie Geiger Johnson and Samuel Louis Johnson, former sharecroppers who came through the Great Depression. They worked the land and saved enough money to acquire their own farm after Lonnie was born in 1947. He was the first son of Lonnie Lee Edwards and his wife Frances, also Mississippi sharecroppers.

Lonnie Lee and Frances Edwards

Born in the segregated south, seven years before The Brown v The Board of Education decision in Topeka, Kansas, Lonnie's arrival in this world on November 7, 1947, came at the end of the harvest season for his parents. Lonnie Lee and Frances were workers of the land, who like parents of their era, operated with limited resources with no paid time off work, nor healthcare, nor prenatal care.

As Frances' water broke, she and Lonnie Lee took the eighteen-mile trek by car over unpaved, gravel roads to the nearest black hospital, passing three small towns in route.

Abbie Geiger Johnson

Six months after Lonnie was born, his grandparents, Samuel Louis and Abbie Johnson, changed the course of their family history forever. In 1948, they took the $1,800 they had saved from years of sharecropping and bought one hundred acres of farmland. No time for Lonnie to be crawling on the couch as the family now had become landowners, establishing roots in the rich Mississippi Delta. All hands would be required to be on deck for this undertaking. The family came together collectively to farm the land. Abbie and Samuel, their five daughters --- Minnie, Frances, Annette, Ruby, Bertha --- and son, Samuel Louis Jr., along with Abbie's siblings and cousins, became full-time farmers on their own land. Most of the work involved tilling the soil, planting cotton and other crops for food before the farm animal acquisitions. With all hands working the land and Lonnie walking, yet not old enough to go to school, his journey into the world of farm work with the family, from sunup until sundown, began with occasional naps on nearby cotton sacks. His being pulled through the fields was an eye-opening experience.

Living on the farm, Lonnie came to know few days of frivolity once he started walking. Playing in the dirt took on a new meaning as a working farmhand. Helping the family eke out a living was to become a full-time job. Lonnie spent those early years in the dirt planting, harvesting crops, and feeding the farm animals. "All hands" included his two little ones as well from sunup until sundown. There was always work to do, even after he entered school.

Johnson Family Farm, Shaw, MS

Rows of cotton growing … ready to be picked!

Hansell Gunn Sr.

Clytee Townsend Gunn

While Lonnie was crawling and getting acclimated to life on his grandmother's farm, a year or so later, on the other side of the state, seemingly thousands of cotton fields away, but really, only a hundred and thirty miles northeast of Shaw, another little black boy was clawing his way into the world as a young black couple was in the birthing room. Two young sharecroppers were awaiting the arrival of their first child. Clytee Townsend Gunn lay in bed, fully ripen, and ready to burst with her husband, Hansell Gunn, Sr., standing nearby while she was travailing in pain.

They were in the back room of a one-bedroom shotgun house that belonged to Louisa Mae Gunn, Hansell Sr.'s mother.

This tiny living space was new for Clytee. While fighting labor pains, she drifted away to a time when her life was not so challenging.

Louisa Mae Gunn

She reflected on growing up on her dad's, Willie Townsend's, one hundred- and ten-acre farm in Una, Mississippi. Her dad was a provider. He inherited about fifty acres of land from his father, raised his brood of thirteen on it, and through hard work, careful planning, and shrewd dealings, purchased an additional sixty acres. In the process, he built a name for himself and found status among white people, who, when addressing him, referred to him as, "Mr. Willie." Clytee was somebody; Mr. Willie's daughter and was treated with respect. But her life was a long way from that now. This nineteen-year-old, soon-to-be mother was light years away from home. She was with her young, twenty-one-year-old husband with barely any room to stretch her legs.

"Mr. Willie" Townsend

A midwife was on hand as the young couple with limited means, no doctor, no prenatal care, and the only nearby hospital serving white people was seven miles away in Okolona, Mississippi. Black midwives attended the needs in the tiny town of five hundred black people in Egypt, Mississippi. In such times, and even today, in rural communities, people make do with what they have --- each other, and the Gunn's were no exception. Clytee was now alone in Egypt, not surrounded by her parents and siblings, and growing up in a hurry.

So, on a chilly January 29th in 1949, Clytee had her first child at home, delivering a healthy seven-pound, chestnut brown, baby boy with long stringy legs. Hansell Gunn, Jr. tested the range on his larynx, screaming after feeling a lash and, obliging the midwife, announcing his arrival. Egypt's population was now five hundred and one.

Hansell came into the world not knowing his arrival came on the heels of the birth of abolitionist, Harriet Tubman, the great liberator of slaves. She, too, entered the world in bondage some one hundred and twenty years earlier. While a lot of things were spiraling about, Hansell could care less. He opened his eyes to a world different from his college friend, Lonnie, who he would meet later in life. He saw hundreds of plantation row houses where black people lived and signs on the other side of the road that he did not understand but said "Whites Only." Early on, Hansell would see Mr. Duc, a white man, telling groups of black men what to do, using a harsh tone to bark out directions. At the time, that did not mean much to him because all he knew was that he was hungry and his mama, Clytee, was right there where he needed her, along with his excited daddy who was a fingertip away. All was good as Hansell snuggled up on Clytee, oblivious to anything else.

Those carefree days were not long enough for Hansell. Even before he was walking, he was introduced to farm life in

A row of shotgun houses similar to the Gunn's home.

Egypt. That life was on Jacque Dermot's farm. While slavery had not existed in America for over eighty years, clearly some shades and facsimiles of it had remained in Egypt. Black people in Egypt no longer wore chains and were not subject to being whipped by their masters but were disenfranchised in every way. The Dermots, a white family, owned everything in Egypt, lock, stock, and barrel --- from the land, the stores, and the food, to the houses in which Hansell and his family lived. Hansell discovered early, that if you did not work for Mr. Dermot, you could neither work nor live in Egypt.

Cotton sacks much like the ones used by Hansell's parents and upon which he rode

Clytee and Hansell Sr. were farm workers. Hansell spent his young years clinging to his mother, who he saw firsthand planting seeds for crops in the spring and chopping weeds around cotton in the summer. He rode on his backside, taking turns on his mom's and dad's cotton sacks looking up and between what he thought were giant trees, but which were really cotton stalks and rows of cotton blocking out his view of the sun. He listened to the scratching sounds of his parents' cotton sacks being dragged along the ground for what seemed like miles and days.

Chapter 2
A Silver Lining Amidst Adversity

Lonnie J. Edwards

School introduced Lonnie to a world outside the farm. He welcomed the change, but the diversion was cut short as a result of a fire. Lonnie's first elementary school was destroyed. The black community was forced to turn to their local church and become the "village" needed to raise and educate their children.

The deaths of Lonnie's grandfather, Samuel Louis Johnson, Sr., and the brutal murder of Emmett Till further created uncertainty and turmoil around his life on the farm. What was certain, though, was that Lonnie's days on the farm were nearing an end. Although he had many hurdles to overcome, Grandma Abbie took him to church, keeping him God-centered. She taught Lonnie his Easter speech, how to pray, and how to care and show support to others. Sunday church was a staple part of his diet. Lonnie never thought it strange growing up, but he could not help noticing that there were white churches and black churches, but no churches with blended congregations. He simply figured that God was everywhere.

Although Lonnie had a steady diet of church, it did not stop him from finding the time to daydream of becoming a professional basketball player. That dream ironically came about after his mother, Frances, left the farm intermittently to work in Chicago. She sent money to help her mother, Abbie, with the farm after the death of her father, Samuel Louis Johnson, Sr. Frances also sent money to her mother to buy her boys a television, after she discovered they were going over to a nearby neighbor's house to watch theirs.

Watching programs on the television opened Lonnie's world, leading him out of isolation. Now, suddenly, he was seeing black men in a different light, celebrated. They were playing basketball and were famous. Lonnie now had his first heroes beyond his grandparents and uncle Samuel Louis Johnson Jr. aka Bunt. He and Bunt, working together, cut down a tree, stuck it in the hard Delta clay, and took off part of the barn door to make him a goal and backboard. They placed it in front of the barn and in back of Abbie's butter bean garden.

Lonnie would practice after school and farm chores, shooting jump shots by the moonlight, on his homemade goal. The farm had no exterior lighting. Eventually, Lonnie would catch the eyes of "Big Cuz," his Uncle James Rodges, who coached the boys' basketball team at McEvans High School. Big Cuz would stop and play one-on-one with Lonnie. The battles would become epic as the student, at fourteen, finally beat the teacher and became ready to try out for the school's team.

Lonnie's love for the game of basketball and the adoration of his siblings kept him grounded. He also had a steady dose of farm chores which kept him humble and taught him how to multi-task. Lonnie had adjusted to sunup and sundown days. However, after his grandmother Abbie passed in 1963, he began spending less time on the farm as his mother began renting the land out.

Freedom from the land did not mean free time as both Lonnie and his brother, Billy, went to work on Fridays after school at his mom's ice cream stand in downtown Shaw. The boys enjoyed working; however, the profits were slim, as her sons ate more food than they sold!

Saturdays were even busier for Lonnie as a community barber. He cut his siblings' hair as well as that of other kids from school. Although Lonnie considered his barbering as a business, the young Entrepreneur gave free haircuts to those who did not have any money. He would be the first to tell you that "his life was no crystal stair," but his grandma Abbie taught him the importance of helping others.

While Grandma Abbie's passing was very painful for Lonnie as he lost his first mentor, it was also a positive turning point in his life. He made the McEvans High School's varsity basketball team, coached by his uncle, Big Cuz. As a Freshman, Lonnie did not get much playing time, but he and Big Cuz knew that was going to change. Lonnie's jump shot showed tremendous promise, and his fire for the game could not be extinguished. As his freshman year climaxed, he showed promise as a two-sport athlete, excelling in both basketball and baseball. But Big Cuz kept him focused on his best skill --- basketball.

Chapter 3
Beginning A New Life on Granddaddy's Farm

Over in Egypt, MS, life for Hansell was beginning to change as he was becoming too big to take naps on his parents' cotton sacks. As he grew, he soon realized that his parents' financial condition and living arrangements were taking a toll on his mom and dad. Living in his dad's mother's cramped shotgun row house was now overcrowded. His dad was no *Willie Townsend*; neither were most men in that day. Hansell Sr. was his mother's youngest, and when he came of age,

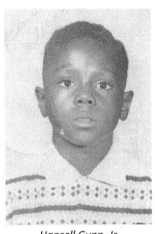

Hansell Gunn, Jr.

he was still living in the nest. All that he knew was in Egypt, the place where he worked and lived – in his mother's home. Consequently, he did not have any long-range plans, and he knew that did not sit well with his new father-in-law. Despite the reservations of her father, Clytee married the man she loved and was determined to stick it out during these tough times.

The years went by, and tough times got tougher after Hansell was born. His sister, Barbara, came along the very next year. With another mouth to feed, now two babies were crammed into this already too tiny living space. Hansell would hear his parents arguing; what about, he did not know. What he did know was that the arguments were happening with a greater frequency. For Hansell, this was unnerving, but the regularity of the arguments had become a normal part of his life. By the time Hansell was six, the tiny house was overrun with children as Clytee now had her third child, his brother, Herbert, in her arms. The arguments with Hansell, Sr. had finally come to a head.

Clytee and Hansell Sr. sat down with their children and told them they were divorcing, splitting up. The children remained with their mother. Divorce was a strange concept for the children as neither Clytee nor Hansell Sr. had enough money to pay for that. They barely had enough funds to feed themselves and their children.

With the divorce, Clytee moved back to her parents' home. All Hansell knew was that the arguments would stop; he would no longer live in that tiny one room house; there was plenty of wide- open space on his granddaddy's farm; there would be a lot of children to play with, cousins everywhere; and he would still see his dad from time to time.

Uncle James Townsend, Hansell's maternal grandfather

Moving to granddaddy's farm in Una, MS meant three things for Hansell: 1) the end of his carefree days of leisure, laying on cotton sacks; 2) an introduction to the world of work; and 3) his finally going to school. Hansell immediately entered the family business from sunup until sundown.

His uncle, James Townsend, was his first teacher on the farm, showing him how to use the two mules, Gee and Haa, to plow the farmland. They would become regulars in his early life.

While Hansell was too young to hook up the plow, he became an expert in following along behind the mules and steadying them for plowing rows during planting season.

James Townsend, Maternal Uncle

When planting season ended, Hansell was further thrown into the world of work. He was pelted by the sweltering heat of the Mississippi sun, which seemed to hang so low, hovering over his head as he chopped weeds from around the cotton he had planted and cultivated. This six-year-old was doing men's work with the long hours, blisters, and the sweat to prove it. With the onset of the Fall, Hansell's work schedule did not get any lighter as he picked cotton and fed the livestock, all before going off to school. As Clytee took employment outside the farm at the Bryan Brothers Meat Cannery, canning potted meat and Vienna sausage, Hansell, her baby boy, was becoming a man. Hansell Sr. left Egypt, MS for Chicago, IL to pursue other work opportunities.

Without much relief, the overcrowded issues continued for Hansell, but now at school in Mrs. Lunette Collin's one room schoolhouse at Pleasant Plain Church School. His classroom housed students grades one through eight. His world was still all black as his school experience was entrenched in segregation.

Hansell took advantage of the overcrowding as he was not a complainer. During his days in Mrs. Collin's classroom, instruction was short with mostly play time. He went home after twelve for lunch and did not return because he had to work on the farm for the rest of the day. Working on the farm often overrode going to school and determined the length of the school day. Hansell spent the first and second grades with Mrs. Collins in that one-room schoolhouse where he felt loved by his teacher and didn't know what he was missing. He was in for a surprise by the third grade.

For Hansell, entering the third grade at Northside School was like awakening from a coma with a heightened sense of awareness. He was no longer in Una, where going to school was no more than a pit stop on his way to granddaddy's farm.

His mother, Clytee had remarried, and her new husband, Fred Ballard, moved the family to the D-1 Jim Jones Court Project Apartments in West Point, MS. He was in the city. This was an upgrade for Hansell as his days of isolation, living on the farm, had abruptly come to an end. For the first time in his young life, school would help him see himself in the mirror, and he didn't like what he saw.

Fred Ballard, Hansell's Stepfather

Hansell had left the safety and anonymity of being in Ms. Collins' overcrowded one-room schoolhouse where he played more than he learned, during the morning hours. The afternoons were spent back at the farm, which was the higher priority. Granddad Townsend put every family member to work, and Hansell was no exception. Now, at his new school,

a new reality set in as he soon discovered that he did not measure up to his peers in his age group.

One day in class, this became clear as he began doing a math problem at the board and was counting by using his fingers. Hansell was mortified to hear his classmates' laughter and to their calling him "dumb." No one had ever put him down before.

Even though his teacher reprimanded his classmates, those words and that teasing would stay with Hansell for a long time. He sensed that he was different; less than his classmates, all of whom were black. The teasing caused Hansell to become self-conscious, but he was determined to correct this glaring inadequacy. With the help of his teachers and his own hard work, Hansell began to surpass those classmates, his critics, by the fifth grade.

Hansell's passion for learning was ignited by the time he entered Fifth Street High School as his confidence had grown and his sense of awareness was even more heightened. In fact, with relentless determination and Townsend pride, he began to excel in his classroom studies!

What also grew over this span of time was his love for sports. He immersed himself into baseball and basketball, and his hard work paid off.

Chapter 4
For The Love of The Game

McEvans High School, Shaw, MS

Making the varsity basketball team spiked an improvement in Lonnie's attendance at school because he was able to spend more time there and less time on the farm. His love for school began to blossom as his playing basketball was directly tied to his academic performance. Frances, his mother, had a "no pass, no play" rule long before the National Collegiate Athletic Association (NCAA) established theirs! Lonnie had teachers who did not give him an academic discount because he was a star player.

There were significant people in those early years who helped to prepare him for his journeys ahead. Someone said, "Behind every successful man, there is a strong woman." Lonnie would agree. The women "pushing" Lonnie were his mom, grandmother, and a host of aunts and teachers. He was once asked, "Why weren't you on the honor roll in high school?" He politely replied, "I averaged missing 30 days a year out of school, picking cotton on the family farm, and I was glad to be on somebody's school roll when I returned."

McEVANS TIGERS

Coach James Rodges (Uncle James/Big Cuz)   *Lonnie on front row, left with jacket*

Lonnie's jump shot caught fire the next three years. As a sophomore, he ranked in the top three players on the team in scoring. This performance would continue throughout his junior and senior years where he averaged twenty plus points each game and made the conference All-Star Team twice. Lonnie's jump shot led him off Gilbert Road and ignited his journey to find his place in life after high school graduation.

Lonnie J. Edwards,
High School Graduation

Along the journey, Lonnie hit some bumps in the road that helped to steady his focus. He earned scholarships to attend several colleges, including Tougaloo, Rust, Mississippi Industrial College, and Mississippi Valley State. Lonnie opted out of attending Mississippi Industrial because he did not want to pursue a technical program. He decided against attending Rust because it was too far to go, and he had no friends attending there.

So, with a lot of thought and discussions, Lonnie and a high school basketball teammate agreed to enroll in Tougaloo in the Fall of 1966. The classmate went to Chicago for the summer, and upon his return to Shaw, he told Lonnie that he had decided not to go to college. Disappointed, but determined that college was in his future, Lonnie went to Tugaloo to enroll, but found that the admissions deadline for the Fall semester had passed. He could not get in!

Feeling dejected, Lonnie talked with the McEvans High School football coach, Herman Smith, about his college situation. At the last minute, Coach Smith got him a tryout with the basketball team at Mississippi Valley State during the late admissions period. His performance earned him a scholarship there, and he enrolled. Lonnie's career at Mississippi Valley State showed promise as he was identified as the most improved player on the team. However, his time there was short-lived, lasting only a semester before Lonnie found himself suspended and out of school for being in an off-limits area on campus. He was devastated and quickly realized how a dream can be shattered to pieces over an unwise decision. For the first time in his young life, Lonnie was on the outside looking in --- out of school --- and without a basketball scholarship, from his perspective, he was facing a bleak future.

Left to Right Row 1: F. Robinson #22, J. Buck #20, L. Oakman #32, Coach J. Neal, W. Washington #12, F. Brandon #14, L. Edwards #24, Row 2: A. Steel #34, R. Ferguson #44, A. McCall #10, A. Spiva #21, E. West #23, Row 3: I. Peterson #52, O. Sparkman #50, E. Credit #50, J. Knighten #15, D. Wyatt #12, E. Pugh #30.

1967 Mississippi Valley State Men's Basketball Team - Lonnie Edwards #24 – Front row

Chapter 5
A Star Is Born

Varsity Basketball Team

Harold scores 2 points against
Starkville

Hansel in action against
Amory

Upon entering high school, Hansell hit his stride. He grew into an athletic frame and became a two-sport athlete, playing both baseball and basketball. Hansell made the varsity basketball team as a freshman and was considered a rising star. His passion for baseball came from his father who loved and played the game as a kid and as a young adult.

Hansell loved to listen to his dad's stories about playing the game. When Hansell lived on his granddad's farm and had completed his chores, he would almost always have a stick in his hand, fantasizing that it was a baseball bat and that he was Jackie Robinson hitting a home run.

Hansell embraced life as student-athlete in high school. His popularity with his peers soared. By his senior year, he was voted "Most Popular

Senior Superlative
"Most Athletic Boy"

Athlete" by his classmates. There was no denying it, Hansell's star was on the rise.

When the summer ended, Hansell's journey continued as he excelled in two sports --- baseball and basketball. He made the varsity teams in each. The boys' baseball team, for the most part, was subpar with, at best, a 9-11 record, but Hansell's right field play, speed, and uncanny ability to get a hit and get on base made him a shining star. He became an All-Star three years in a row despite never being exposed to a formal baseball camp nor having any training to read signs used by experienced coaches. Hansell's love for the game was passed down to him from his father who was a natural in right field.

Even though baseball was Hansell's passion, he made his mark with basketball. He made the Fifth Street Bombers High School's boys' basketball team in his freshman year. By Hansell's senior year, in 1967, his team went down to the state championships with a 27- 6 record. He led all scorers on the team, averaging thirty-five points per game. Hansell's performances during his first two seasons earned him scholarship offers from nearby Mary Holmes Junior College and Coahoma Junior College.

Hansell Gunn, Jr.
Senior Class Salutatorian

He graduated high school as the class Salutatorian, and he committed to attending Coahoma after meeting with Coach "Pop" Gaines.

Reflecting upon his early days as the little boy at the blackboard, counting on his fingers and being laughed at by his classmates, Hansell felt very accomplished. Those days seemed like light years away.

Chapter 6
Coahoma: A New Beginning Leads to Unchartered Territories

Time away from the court gave Lonnie an opportunity to return to his farm roots and to reconnect with a childhood friend, W.C. Peterson. Peterson worked at Denton's Dairy in Cleveland, Mississippi and attended Coahoma Junior College nearby. One day, while at Coahoma, Peterson spoke to the coach about Lonnie. Coach Gaines was aware of Lonnie's high school performance, and after they met and discussed his college situation, Coach gave Lonnie a positive nod, and he transferred to Coahoma. He was given a fresh start. So, Coahoma's men's basketball team rolled into the second semester with a new arrival making his presence known.

Coahoma was a new beginning for Lonnie and his presence there during the second semester changed the landscape. All of the players were jockeying for a position on the team. Lonnie was hungry to prove that he belonged on the basketball court and was ready for all comers. For him, that meant that he was not going to take it easy on anyone.

Lonnie Edwards - #24 – playing with the Coahoma Tigers

Under Coach Pop Gaines, Lonnie learned from his mistakes and excelled at Coahoma, both as a student and as an athlete. He fought a fellow teammate, Earnest Killum, for control of the team.

Neither gave an inch as their battles in practice showed their
dominance and pushed Hansell further down on the depth
chart. With Lonnie putting the hours in on the court and
curtailing his social life off the court, he developed
academically as a student and became an exceptional Team
Captain during his Sophomore year, averaging 20+ points per
game. During that season, Coahoma averaged more than 20
wins with Lonnie leading the team in scoring, on defense, and
in post-season play.

Lonnie received scholarship offers to attend the University of
Kansas as well as to several other colleges. However, he
heeded the advice of Coach Pop Gaines --- to accept a
scholarship to become the first black male student-athlete on
the campus of Alabama College, an institution of higher
education in Montevallo, Alabama. His decision to leave
Coahoma for Alabama College came as a result of a lot of
soul searching. After all, it was a college with almost all white
students and staff, and Lonnie had never lived in that type of
setting.

Montevallo's Coach Bill Jones scouted Coahoma Junior
College's basketball program, attending games with a mission
to look for and find an exceptional athlete and student who
could show his basketball program how to win as well as to
integrate the school and their basketball conference without
igniting a civil rights situation. Coach Jones wanted a change
agent who could help bring his college in compliance with the
federal guidelines. He wanted a champion with style,
charisma, and discipline who could help grow the Alabama
Collegiate Conference and their school communities. While at
Coahoma, Coach Jones met an exemplary African American
student athlete who he felt would bridge the gap between
black and white people by becoming that agent for positive
change. So, after much thought and many discussions, he
offered Alabama College's first basketball scholarship for a
male student-athlete of color to Lonnie J. Edwards.

After accepting the scholarship, Lonnie packed his bags,
carrying along his lone pair of white Allstar tennis shoes, his

refined jump shot, a sack lunch from his Coahoma coach, and the confidence that if it was to be, it would be up to him to make a difference. When he entered Alabama College in the fall of 1969, it had been renamed the University of Montevallo on September 1st. Lonnie could not have known that his Montevallo experience would lead to a future that included his being regarded as one of the *silent integrators*!

The University of Montevallo (Alabama College) - Montevallo, AL 1969

First visit to the University Campus
(L-R) Eddie Johnson, Lonnie Edwards, Billy Williams, Hansell Gunn, Jr.,
Coach Bill Jones, Bill Rountree, and Herman Watts

Chapter 7
A Bright Spot in The Shadows

The cheers of "Hansell, Hansell" all but disappeared after Hansell transitioned to Coahoma Junior College in the Fall of his freshman year. He quickly discovered that the college had no baseball team. Thus, basketball would be his only outlet. Hansell's star basketball status had been replaced by the harsh reality of anonymity. In high school, he was a big fish in a small pond. However, at Coahoma, Hansell was the guppy swimming upstream against a rapid tide. His new teammates, Earnest Killum, Lonnie Edwards, Sherman Hogan, and Cliff Harris ruled the roost, limiting his playing time and having him relegated to the position as a role player with a good outside shot.

Nevertheless, Hansell remained on the team and was an exceptional outside threat as was noticeably clear in his second year, after Killum transferred to Stetson University in DeLand, Florida. In a key game against Utica College, the Coahoma team, minus a big man in the post position and with Lonnie sitting on the bench in foul trouble, found themselves at risk of losing. But, the coach, Pop Gaines, called on Hansell to do what he recruited him to do --- to score. Hansell had a blowout game, raining outside jumpers and keeping the team on a winning roll. Then, Lonnie came off the bench and hit a long- range jumper, sending the game into overtime. It was all Hansell in the overtime, scoring twenty-five points, and leading Coahoma to a victory!

When Hansell's sophomore season ended, he had plans of attending Jackson State University in Jackson, Mississippi to pursue opportunities in both baseball and basketball. However, a chance trip with his teammate, Lonnie Edwards, to Alabama College to sign his Letter of Acceptance derailed his plans.

Alabama College had prepared to offer only one basketball scholarship to a Coahoma student – to Lonnie Edwards. So, Hansell did not feel any pressure to perform. He and another teammate, Billy Williams, toured the campus and took part in workouts with the team. Hansell enjoyed his visit, but did not give it much thought since, at the time, he was not being recruited. However, a telephone call to Pop Gaines a couple of months later changed all that.

Coach Gaines had been in contact with Coach Jones of Alabama College and was informed that a second scholarship was available for another Coahoma student to go with Lonnie. When Coach Gaines shared this news with Lonnie, as one might imagine, he was excited that he was not going to Alabama College alone. He met with Coach Gaines and agreed with him that the second scholarship should be awarded to Hansell Gunn, Jr.

Who's Who in American Junior Colleges
Eighteen Coahomans, including Hansell and Lonnie, were chosen from their graduating class to join an elite group of student leaders selected from 600 colleges in all 50 states, the District of Columbia.

Selections were based on scholarship, leadership in extracurricular activities, service to the community and future potential.

30 years

Thirty years of players and coaches watched the Basketball Homecoming contests at Coahoma Community College and Agricultural High School this past weekend. Three coaches were presented with plaques from their players during halftime ceremonies. Seated from left are Arthur Fielder who coached from the mid '70's to the '80's, William "Pop" Gaines who coached what some term the "Golden Years" from 1964-'73, and longtime football coach and Athletic Director George Green. Behind them are players from their teams who made the presentations.

The faculty, staff, and coaches at Coahoma Junior College (now Coahoma Community College), along with many of the local community residents provided the guidance and support as well as the academic and athletic preparation for Lonnie and Hansell to succeed at the University of Montevallo. It was their springboard and they will be forever grateful for it.

Chapter 8
Confronting Childhood Fears

When Lonnie told Hansell of his scholarship opportunity, he was stunned at the news and intrigued too. He never had a close relationship with white people, and now he had to choose between attending the historically black college and university (HBCU) he dreamed of --- Jackson State University --- and the prospect of satisfying his curiosity about coexisting with white people. While making his decision, Hansell's mind drifted back to his work experience at the Bryan Brothers' Meat Cannery. He couldn't help but notice the distinct separation of the races. Black people were the laborers, and white people were the supervisors. For Hansell, it was shades of being that five-year-old boy again and watching Mr. Duc back in Egypt. There he grew up seeing him lauding his authority over the black workers. It was normal for the times and locale, but it was never really settling for young Hansell, Jr.

As a teen, Hansell worked strictly with other black people. He saw young white males, watching them from a distance, but there was no interaction with them. He could not help but feel that something was wrong with this separation as he continued to work, talking only to his black coworkers. As he ate and talked, he was careful not to share his uneasy feeling with his peers. Hansell knew about the unwritten rules among his peers about interacting with and talking to white people.

Emmett Till

Hansell was five years old when the story about Emmett Till's violent murder in Money, Mississippi broke in 1955. The actions by that angry mob of white people sent ripples throughout black communities and, unfortunately, stayed with Hansell. It served as a reminder to black people not to get too close to white people. This murder kept Hansell's antennas on high alert. He remained guarded about his thoughts and feelings so as not to reveal them to anyone, especially outside his family as they would create potential problems. Hansell did not like the feelings he was having towards white people because he knew that he had no personal encounters to justify them.

Hansell went to church every Sunday with granddaddy, and he was taught to love everybody. All that he knew was that he was jaded by what happened in Money, Mississippi, and he could not shake it. Hansell knew that he was painting all white people with broad strokes, and deep down, he hoped that he would let go of those preconceptions, but he just did not know how. His lack of communication and direct contact with white people fed into his fears and distrust. One day, Hansell thought, this would change; but he did not know when.

After completing his Associates degree at Coahoma Junior College, an unforeseen opportunity was placed in Hansell's lap. He received a phone call from Coach Gaines, informing him that Lonnie would call him about a scholarship possibility. In Lonnie's call, he told Hansell that Coach Jones from Alabama College had offered a second full basketball scholarship to a Coahoma student and asked if he was interested in taking it.

Hansell shared the news with his family and weighed their input as he made his decision. The negatives against Alabama College and the fear of white people were huge hurdles. However, Hansell reflected upon his positive experience at Lonnie's signing, particularly the scrimmage with the team. All players looked forward to scrimmages because it was their chance to compete and show their skills.

While playing ball on a visit at Alabama College, Hansell had a strange thing to happen to him while they were playing ball. He noticed a small, older white man sitting on the bleachers at the far end of the gymnasium. He had white hair, a white beard, and he wore a blue, checkered jacket. During a break from playing, Hansell went into the hallway to get a drink from the water fountain. As he turned to walk back into the gym, he looked directly into the eyes of this mysterious older man.

According to Hansell, he had the strangest, deepest, darkest eyes he had ever seen! It appeared that his eyes were completely full of blackness. The man stared at him for about 20 seconds, and when he spoke, he said, "You know Alabama College has a reputation of being one of the best schools in the state. It has a history of preparing people for successful careers. If YOU can weather the storm, there will be numerous opportunities awaiting you. These are terrible times! There will be difficult days ahead! You will be challenged like you have never been challenged before."

He kept emphasizing "terrible times." He went on to say, "There will be those who will talk about you for the stand you take. There will be those who will stab you in the back because of hate and greed. Don't quit! Don't give up! Don't allow the world to steal your dream." He then turned and slowly walked away. When he left, Hansell said that it seemed as if he was finally released from a trance. He said that he never saw the man again, even though he searched for him in the building after the scrimmages. Hansell described him to other people there, but no one he asked had seen or knew anyone fitting the description of this man. So, he thought, "Was he an Angel sent with a special message for me?"

Hansell did not tell anyone about the message from the stranger because, at that time, he had no intention of attending Alabama College. He had a full scholarship to attend Jackson State University in Jackson, MS and was looking forward to enrolling there.

Nevertheless, Hansell hung on to that encounter with the stranger he met while drinking water from the fountain in the hallway. The words of wisdom given him by the enigmatic older man who told him that enrolling in

Alabama College would enrich his life was one of the reasons he signed the scholarship and made the decision to enroll in Alabama College. Attending school there offered the prospect of playing baseball again, which also interested him. So, Hansell joined Lonnie in the Fall of their junior year as one of the first two black male athletes to attend Alabama College, which had changed its name to the University of Montevallo. He became the second *silent integrator*.

Chapter 9
A Change is Coming!

Four years prior to Lonnie Edwards' and Hansell Gunn's arrival on the campus of Alabama College, the wheels of change were set in motion.

In 1965, the board of trustees of Alabama College authorized President D.P. Culp to sign the Certificates of Assurance of Compliance with the Civil Rights Act of 1964. In the fall of 1968, three African American women, Carolyn Burpo, Ruby Kennbrew and Dorothy (Lilly) Turner, enrolled in the university. In the fall of 1969, Lonnie J. Edwards and Hansell Gunn, Jr. enrolled as the first African American student-athletes.

The grand plan devised by Dr. Leon Davis, Montevallo's Athletic Director and Former Head Coach of the college's men's basketball teams, was finally coming to fruition. Dr. Davis and the new men's basketball Head Coach, Bill Jones, scouted Lonnie playing basketball for the first time in the southern classic where his all-black Coahoma Junior College team played against and defeated a white team. Dr. Davis was impressed with Coahoma's performance during the game in Gulfport, MS and even more so with Lonnie when the awards were being given out.

Lonnie had an extraordinary level of personal performance, and although he was among the top scorers in the three games played, with 59 total points, he was not selected for the All-Tournament team. In addition, although Lonnie's team won the Championship game, his team was not afforded the accolades which normally accompanied the winning team. Tournament representatives only selected one player from the winning team to be named to the All-Tournament team, and it was not Lonnie. In fact, the player from the Coahoma team was the only black player named to the All- Tournament team. It seemed that the tournament representatives made more "to do" about the white players from the losing teams.

Despite it all, Lonnie and the Coahoma Junior College team were the real stars that night. They handled themselves in an exemplary fashion, considering their overt slighting by the tournament organizers. Dr. Davis was convinced by Lonnie's demeanor and professionalism in handling that blatantly unfair situation that he would be the right fit for Alabama College.

On the bus ride back to Coahoma, Coach Gaines continuously gave Lonnie encouraging words, with several pats on the knee. He said such things as, "Don't let the unfairness of the situation get you down, son" and "Remember, you are already selected for the All-SIC Conference team." While the blatant snub still hurt, Lonnie was able to get past it and focus on his future.

The next chapter in his future began at the University of Montevallo.

Chapter 10
Playing Through Dissension

Lonnie's prowess and his lone pair of Fred Dollar Store All Star Converse tennis shoes quietly integrated a predominantly white university. He set out to improve race relations without a boycott or marching in the streets. Upon entering Montevallo, Lonnie's expectations were high based on Coach Jones' recruitment of him. He expected to make an impact right away. However, little did he know that this was just the beginning of his destiny as one of the *silent integrators*.

Lonnie's and Hansell's arrival on the University of Montevallo's campus was without the negative scenes which were often occurring with students enrolling in all-white colleges around the country, as there was no governor and no angry mob baring their access or entry to the campus. The media didn't even show up. Lonnie and Hansell knew things would be different, but so far, it was uneventful. Lonnie thought to himself, "Surely integration isn't going to be this easy!"

The two Coahoma grads had never been close friends before enrolling at Montevallo. At Coahoma, other than being basketball teammates, they were more like passing strangers. Each traveled in different circles, with different sets of friends. Hansell was the introvert and somewhat of a recluse. Lonnie, also known as "Road Dog," was the extrovert. He was outgoing and a team/campus celebrity.

The legend of Road Dog began at McEvans High School and grew with more stories from Coahoma Junior College based on Lonnie's averaging, at both institutions, 20+ points per game and leading the teams to post-season play with back-to-back 20-win seasons.

Lonnie's easy, calm demeanor made him a heavily celebrated recruit. But now, circumstances dictated that he would have to modify his behavior as he and Hansell would have to learn to lean and to depend on each other. They had more in common than before as they were now the new "minorities" on a college campus that was bigger than their hometowns. They also would share a dorm room and together face new challenges that others on the campus would not have.

To help the University of Montevallo comply with the federal requirements for funding mandates and to do so without marches in the streets and boycotting, Lonnie was chosen as one of their ambassadors for change. It was almost as if he served as their "Jackie Robinson." How ironic that the year in which Lonnie was born, 1947, was the same year Robinson entered Major League Baseball. However, unlike Robinson's, Lonnie's step onto the integrated stage was not covered extensively by the media, but it was scrutinized, nevertheless, by the white and black college communities.

Lonnie was instrumental in giving the University of Montevallo the first of two winning basketball seasons and with it, more collegiate pride. During this same time, Lonnie gained enhanced life skills, a high-quality education, and the expertise and confidence necessary to later integrate and lead a school district.

Montevallo was "no crystal stair" as both Lonnie and Hansell contended with some unwanted challenges as "the gloves came off," so to speak, first, with their new white teammates. In one of the first basketball games of the season, Coach Jones found himself appeasing the white parents by having Lonnie "come off the bench," instead of having him in the team's starting 5 players. Clearly, this did not sit well with Lonnie, having been the Team Captain wherever he played. Having white athletes, not as skilled or talented, starting over him and getting more playing time was a bit too much to swallow.

Prior to the regular season's first basketball game, Coach Jones met Lonnie at a local restaurant to discuss his playing on the team and told him that he was pleased with his preseason performance. But he brought to Lonnie's attention that he had five (5) seniors who had been starters for Coach Davis and who expected to be starters for him. Coach shared that he had seen a change in attitudes among the players, causing dissension between his team leaders. He said that he felt that it was largely because of their fear of losing status and playing time if he started him. Lonnie told him that while he did not agree with his decision, he understood.

Chapter 11
The Ultimate Breakthrough

One day at practice, the Montevallo team was running through their traditional plays when Lonnie varied and improvised a play. Immediately, many of the players began yelling, "That wasn't the play, Lonnie!" Then, Coach Jones grabbed Lonnie by his jersey, tearing it and angrily saying, "That was not the play!" Lonnie looked at Coach Jones, took off the torn jersey, threw it to the floor, and kicked it, saying, "We're not winning anyway with these plays!" Without responding, Coach Jones resumed the practice, but it was more physical than usual. A short while later, he ended the practice for the evening.

Early in the regular basketball season, Coach Jones invited two all-black high schools to play each other before the University of Montevallo's varsity game. He was interested in having other black players to join his team. So, to aid in his recruiting efforts, he substituted Lonnie in the starting lineup. It was the seventh game of the season. Lonnie had an exceptional performance that night. He gave the crowd a show, making 25 points! The local newspaper printed, "Lonnie Edwards has broken into the lineup at Montevallo."

Lonnie warming up, pre-game drills

Coach Jones instructing team

On the following Saturday night's game, however, Lonnie was not selected as a starter.

The Montevallo team struggled as Lonnie sat watching from the bench. Things were not going well, and the team was behind. Some of these fans had seen Lonnie's performance earlier in the week, and many had observed him dunking the ball and hitting outside shots during warm-ups. For the crowd, it was shades of preseason when they saw Lonnie lighting it up in the gym. They dreamed of it happening during the regular season. But, so far, that hadn't happened. Finally, they couldn't take it anymore.

So, suddenly, with their team trailing early in the game, the predominately white crowd of fans had a breakout moment chanting, "We want Lonnie! We want Lonnie!" Neither Coach Jones nor Lonnie had heard that chant before from an almost all-white crowd. Lonnie sat on the bench next to Hansell looking around. Hansell asked Lonnie, "Do you hear that?" Lonnie said, "Yeah!" Hansell asked Lonnie, "What are you going to do?" Lonnie replied, "If I get in, I'm going to shoot every time the ball touches my hand." Before Lonnie could finish speaking, Coach Jones ran over and grabbed him, nearly tearing his jersey as he pushed him to the scorer's table.

The die was cast that night. The integration wheel was going full throttle with no looking back. The fans' chant caught Coach Jones' attention.

Lonnie Edwards #14 in flight

Apparently, this was the kind of fuel he needed to make a change. So, he sent Lonnie in to play. He struck the match, setting the gym on fire. The rest of the night, Lonnie launched and hit nothing but long-range jumpers; nothing but net!

The fans didn't see black anymore. They had experienced something new and were not about to let it go. For the first time, Montevallo had their own gym rocking. Lonnie gave the fans what they were hungering for, sweet victory. That night, the Montevallo team won, and their fans embraced Lonnie as their star player. A number of his senior class teammates were disappointed. But they all appeared happy that the team had won.

The next day at practice, Coach Jones called Lonnie out to the center of the gym floor, not for a correction this time. Instead, Coach threw the ball to him and said, "It's your team. Run it!" He made Lonnie a Team Co-Captain. With this change, the team went on a winning streak. Lonnie's play thrilled the fans everywhere, bringing black people on to the campus for the first time to witness the black phenom and to support Montevallo's winning program.

Lonnie Edwards, Team Co-Captain

Suddenly, Montevallo's community was looking united, coming together as one neighborhood. Black people began to attend the basketball games; truly a first. The audience was segregated initially but by the second year everyone sat together. What a sight!

Hansell Gunn, Jr. making the points!

Hansell blocking that shot!

uNiversity of montevallo falcons

INDIVIDUAL RECORDS

Chapter 12
Change Was Not Easy

At the college, although they experienced micro-aggressive behavior from other students as well as from some of their teachers and administrators, general acceptance of Lonnie and Hansell seemed to be increasing. However, it didn't take long for the "proverbial bubble" to burst.

After Lonnie was made the team's Co-Captain, over to the side in the gym, he noticed several independent meetings by senior players. Observing a difference in their behaviors, he reflected on his meeting with Coach Jones. *(Coach Jones told Lonnie that he had five (5) seniors who had been starters for Coach Davis and who expected to be starters for him. He said that he had seen a change in attitudes among the players, causing dissension between his team leaders. He said that he felt that it was largely because of their fear of losing status and playing time if he started Lonnie.)*

Perhaps, coincidently, after Lonnie's elevation to Co-Team Captain, several suspicious incidents took place. Three of them appeared to be specifically designed to frighten the integrators enough to cause them to withdraw from college.

The first incident occurred one evening as Lonnie and Hansell prepared to settle down for the night in their dorm room. A growling sound was heard coming from beneath Hansell's bottom bunk bed. Lonnie and Hansell both became concerned as Hansell lifted the bed cover to find a snarling opossum. For a moment, they were afraid, forgetting that they had spent their early lives on a farm. Opossums, rabbits, and squirrels were generally found outside and were normally on the run as they were hunted for food. However, finding a wild animal under their dorm bed got the young men's attention. Hansell grabbed the broom leaning in one of the corners of their room and chased the critter out of the building. Lonnie would remember this prank but would not let on to their peers that this was a big deal. He chose to see it as an initiation ritual in which they clearly did not want to participate.

Angry opossum

But was there an underlying message associated with the animal someone chose to put in their room? It was an opossum but was it supposed to be a raccoon? Was the opossum the closest, tame animal to a racoon that could be controlled enough to put in the dorm room? Was someone trying to refer to Lonnie and Hansell as "coons" or "possums" or was it just a juvenile prank? *"On postcards black children were often referred to as coons, monkeys, crows, and opossums."* Source: https://www.ferris.edu/jimcrow/coon/

"The 'coon' caricature is one of the most insulting of all anti-black caricatures. The name itself, an abbreviation of raccoon, is dehumanizing.   The coon was portrayed as a lazy, easily frightened, chronically idle, inarticulate, buffoon. The coon acted childish, but he was an adult; albeit a good-for-little adult.

The coon, although he often worked as a servant, was not happy with his status. He was, simply, too lazy, or too cynical to attempt to change his lowly position. By the 1900s, coons were increasingly identified with young, urban blacks who disrespected whites."
Source: https://www.ferris.edu/jimcrow/coon

The second incident also took place in/near Lonnie's and Hansell's dorm room. Late one night, they heard a liquid being poured on the dormitory's hallway floor. Almost immediately, they saw a fire on some of the liquid that seeped underneath the door of their room and smelled smoke as it oozed through the keyhole. Lonnie and Hansell put out the fire in their room and opened a window to clear the smoke instead of running out into the hall right away. When they finally opened the door leading to the hallway, they saw the tile on the floor had burned. They could not help but notice that the fire alarm was not pulled! There was never a mention of the incident by their peers or administrators; no one ever questioned the big, burned spot in front of their dormitory door. To their knowledge, there was never an investigation of the episode. So, Lonnie and Hansell believed that someone was, again, trying to send them a message.

The third incident happened one day when Lonnie was on his way to his dorm after eating lunch in the cafeteria. Walking by the campus' Maintenance Building, he saw a noose hanging from a tree. It was placed high up in the tree and stayed there for more than a week.

Hansell saw it too as he returned to the dorm from baseball practice. Neither discussed it with their peers nor reported it to the administration. Not one person mentioned it to them! Ironically, after hanging there for several days, they noticed that it was gone just as quickly as it appeared. Nevertheless, Lonnie had had enough of this harassment. He decided he was not about to let this offensive, aggressive action go unanswered, not this time; nor would they go crying about it to the school administration. Lonnie felt that someone needed to be held accountable and be taught a lesson.

Since the culprit did not confess and no one else volunteered information to his identity, *everybody* would pay the price. He didn't know how that would happen, but the thought stayed in the recesses of his mind.

Not only did the pranks come, but also subtle intimidation behaviors. After class one day, a student body representative invited Lonnie to come by his apartment to have lunch with him. Lonnie accepted the invitation, but after a few minutes of small talk, the conversation took an uncomfortable turn. The host told Lonnie that he was concerned about what might happen to him based on some of the conversations going around campus. Lonnie asked, "What kind of conversations?" The host said that some people were saying that he was taking white girls in his car to Birmingham and that they were concerned about that. Lonnie first corrected the rumor and stated that he did not have a car. He told the host, "If *some people* are saying that, it is not true." As the host was talking, he was preparing soup to share with Lonnie for lunch. He set the soup bowls down on the counter, giving Lonnie one, and keeping the other for himself. When he turned his back to get something else out of the cabinet, Lonnie switched the bowls. As the host talked more, Lonnie told him to keep the soup, thanked him for sharing the information, and recommended that he put a stop to the rumors since he now knew the truth. He then left the apartment.

The next day, Lonnie shared this conversation with Coach Jones who said that he would address it with the student body representative. He never knew what Coach Jones said to him or what transpired, but after that encounter, Lonnie never saw that student again.

In spite of all of these pranks and intimidation attempts, Lonnie never changed his attitude, temperament, or behavior when interacting with the students. Many later claimed to be his fans and showed it in many ways. Hansell remained more guarded.

Chapter 13
Walls Came Tumbling Down

A few weeks later, on a freezing Alabama night, Lonnie thought of an opportunity for "payback." He crept upstairs from his first-floor dorm room, pulled the fire alarm, and eased back to his room during the ensuing commotion. There, he and Hansell watched the chaos unfold as scantily dressed, white, male bodies ran from inside the warm dormitory to the dark, frosty night outside. They stood shivering in the light of the trucks, as the fire department evacuated the building looking for the non-existent fire. Lonnie and Hansell hid in the warmth of their room, laughing. The next day, Dean Wilkinson questioned them about the fire alarm incident. He mentioned that he did not see them outside with the other students. Lonnie and Hansell jokingly told him that because of their skin color, it was hard to see them at night. No further discussion!

After that incident occurred, things began to settle down and no more hidden surprises surfaced. For Lonnie, that meant the initiation was over for now.

For Hansell, however, the initiation continued, albeit not during basketball season. Baseball season was where he felt the big pinch. It was during this time that Hansell

Hansell Gunn, Jr. with University of Montevallo's Baseball Team

felt alone and vulnerable. He was separated from Lonnie for lengthy periods of time on the road and had no one in which to confide or even relate. Not only was he the only African America in baseball at the University, but he was also the only African American in baseball in the conference!

During Hansell's time on the road as well as at some of the home games, the pressure really heated up. He was a "walk-on" on the baseball team, not a recruit. While he had some skills, his lack of formal training in the nuances of the game resulted in his being behind his teammates in performing. Initially, it was thought that what Hansell lacked in training, would be negated by his speed and his ability to get on base. However, it did not take him long to realize that not having training in reading signs and not having played baseball at the collegiate level were glaring weaknesses.

With Montevallo's baseball team floundering near the bottom in their region and conference, Hansell's mistakes drew more negative attention from the white spectators, fueling his anxieties. He was accustomed to the stares, but those looks changed to boos. At first, that was okay too. But, when the "Home" and "Away" ballpark crowds' boos changed to calls of "Nigger," Hansell became more withdrawn, staying to himself instead of mingling with the team. He felt defeated and even more isolated when his teammates did not standup for him when this happened. The rides home and the walks back to his dorm room after games became long, lonely ones.

Hansell was living alone in this nightmare. He could not tell Lonnie what was happening to him as he did not want to look like a complainer or appear "soft." But quitting was not an option! Nonetheless, it was obvious that his confidence was eroding. For Hansell, this situation was reminiscent of Mr. Duc in Egypt, MS, barking directions at black people who worked in the community. He never understood why he acted that way.

University of Montevallo baseball team - 1967-1968;
Hansell Gunn, Jr. top row, 2nd from right

But Hansell refused to become that quiet little boy again, hiding from the rage inside of him. Instead, it would take a moment, but he would release his fear and regain his confidence.

Hansell began spending extra hours after practice with his white coaches learning how to read baseball signs. These sessions marked the first time he had conversations with white people in which he did not feel awkward or out of place. Hansell became a much better baseball player, and his mistakes decreased. As a result, he started to win the fans over, but in his gut, he still had trust issues with white people. He was willing to address his trust issues, especially when all of the white coaches took their time, without reservations, to ensure he learned the signs and signals to improve his personal performance.

The story of the Silent Integrators cannot be fully told without talking about Montevallo's black community. They were so proud of Hansell and Lonnie and graciously invited them into their homes, usually for Sunday dinners after church. Some of the invitations were clearly attempts to find proper suitors for their daughters!

As one can imagine, there was limited entertainment for young black people in the small community. There was, however, Pearlie's, a Juke Joint, where everyone went on the weekend! The best Barbeque and Fried Fish one has ever eaten was always on the menu. The 'Blues" blasted on the jukebox and the patrons danced the night away. Everyone went to Pearlie's!

Lonnie J. Edwards and Hansell Gunn, Jr.
college students

These student-athletes were treated like Rock Stars whenever they ventured out into the community! However, when back on campus, this celebrity status was quickly gone. Hansell and Lonnie knew they were right back to "looking over their shoulders." What was starting to become clear to them was their perspective on what it meant to have a black man to live and interact with white people.

For Lonnie, evidence of the beginning of their acceptance was ever so clear when one of his white friends had allowed him to borrow his car to get around the city. Lonnie had a great time using his car. But, one day, his friend showed him $150.00 in parking fines that Lonnie had accrued for parking in unauthorized areas and for expired parking meters. Faced with this problem, Lonnie went to the Dean of Students, confessed that the tickets were his, and asked for his help in arranging for him to pay for them. The Dean provided a workable plan for Lonnie to pay his fines, and surprisingly, his friend allowed him to resume driving privileges using his car!

While neither the University of Montevallo nor the town of Montevallo, AL had previously embraced diversity, it was apparent that Lonnie and Hansell were making serious divots into a previously smooth, homogeneous landscape. The frigid climate displayed by the masses of people upon their arrival was summarily melting as the student-athletes started to settle into their new surroundings. Their differences, although obvious, were becoming less important in their treatment.

In fact, on one occasion, Lonnie reciprocated their peers' actions of kindness by allowing one of his white friends to borrow his car. However, a problem arose that did not involve unpaid parking tickets. Lonnie received a call from the police informing him that his car had been involved in an accident. Lonnie's friend who was driving his car was okay, but the other driver smashed the back bumper and the kit. Another white friend allowed Lonnie to borrow his car to go to the accident scene. After arriving at the scene, the officer spoke with Lonnie, found that he was owner of the car, and learned that he was a University of Montevallo basketball player. The situation was resolved with the other motorist being cited for intoxication and allowed to pay damages for Lonnie's vehicle. Lonnie exhaled as an amicable resolution was reached in that matter.

The months passed by and Lonnie and Hansell felt a sense of belonging in the City of Montevallo as they spent time off-campus, familiarizing themselves with their surroundings, and attending high school athletic events. Most of their leisure time was spent observing or participating in activities around the city and in churches.

As each became submerged into the culture at Montevallo, Hansell never knew what Lonnie was going to do in any given situation. Even though they were far from home and growing into adulthood, occasionally, Lonnie would push the envelope by testing the boundaries of racial acceptance. Every now and then, evidence of remaining support for segregation could still be seen.

One day after class, on the way to their dormitory, two white male classmates invited Lonnie to join them in stopping by another dorm to get popcorn. When they entered, there were several white female students in the lobby's living area. They all greeted the young men warmly and asked them to sit and talk with them for a while. After a short while, a new "house mom" came into the lobby, and when she saw Lonnie in the group of students, she looked at him and began shouting, "Get out! Get out! Get out! What are you doing in here? Get out now!" The other students looked in horror and hung their heads in embarrassment, but respecting her authority, they did not speak up for Lonnie nor talk back to her. So, Lonnie got up and left --- alone.

When he got back to the dorm, he told Hansell all about what happened. He told Lonnie, "Man, I've been telling you to stop being so friendly with those people. You are going to get yourself hung!"

The next day, Lonnie told Dr. Davis, the Athletic Director, about the incident. He asked Lonnie, "What did you do when you were told to get out?" He told him that he left. Then, he asked, "What did you say?" Lonnie told him that he did not say anything. He looked pensively for a moment, then told Lonnie that he had done the right thing in that situation. He said that if Lonnie had reacted in a way that was disrespectful or confrontational, he might have been correct in protecting his feelings and his rights, but the situation might have been raised to a level that it could have led to the end of Lonnie's time at the university.

Later that week, Lonnie saw the "dorm mom" in the university's cafeteria. She walked toward him shrugging her shoulders with her hands somewhat raised, mouthing, "I did not know. I did not know." Lonnie nodded his head and kept going. He guessed that she was saying that she did not know that he was one of the star players on the basketball team. But he thought that it should not have mattered in her determination of how to
treat him. Lonnie thought, "I am a human being, just like the other students, and should not have been treated differently. "

One time, Lonnie and Hansell were about twenty miles outside of Montevallo, in the small town of Centreville. Both were hungry and decided to stop at a restaurant serving bar-b-que. Upon exiting the car, Hansell noticed Lonnie was walking towards the front door entrance. He knew that this would be a problem. After all, they were in Alabama of all places. A discussion between the two began as Lonnie told Hansell, "Not today."

When they entered the front door of the restaurant, all patrons' eyes locked in on them while the sounds of the utensils hitting plates as well as all conversations came to an abrupt halt.

Sign common during the Jim Crow era in the South

They both saw the black cooks in the kitchen waving their arms and hands and directing them to come to the back door of the restaurant. But they were ignored.

The restaurant manager fastened his eyes on them and asked where they were from. Hansell gasped and was speechless, not knowing what was going to happen next. It felt like a bad scene in one of his nightmares, but this was no dream; he felt trapped. To his surprise, Lonnie was as cool as if he were releasing a jump shot with seconds left on clock in front of a hostile crowd, hitting nothing but net. Lonnie turned and showed the manager his University of Montevallo letterman's jacket. Attitudes all over the restaurant changed immediately. The manager took their order and escorted them to their table. The patrons' conversations and eating resumed as the two sat down for their meals.

The men's basketball team's fame and Lonnie's and Hansell's contributions to it had now clearly gone beyond the hallowed gym of the University of Montevallo. This simple act of acceptance in a segregated eating establishment epitomizes the strength and impact of the *silent integrators*.

When basketball season came to an end for that year, Lonnie and Hansell returned to their respective homes in Mississippi for Spring Break. They spent the next three days with their families before reuniting in Columbus, MS to head back to Montevallo.

Traveling between Tuscaloosa and Centerville, Alabama where they had picked up some delicious bar-b-que, they ran out of gas! They were about thirty miles outside of Montevallo. Lonnie had overestimated the amount of gas remaining in his little blue Datsun and had passed up a gas station about five miles back thinking that they had enough gas to get back to the college campus. But, alas, their luck ran out and so did the gas! They were stranded on a dark, lonely stretch of highway in Alabama.

Lonnie and Hansell got out of the car and walked the five miles back to the gas station they had passed only to discover that it had closed and would not open again until 7:00 a.m. the next morning. As a result, the two would have to walk five miles back to their car and spend the night in it. This did not sit well with Hansell as he began to reflect upon the murders of three civil rights workers --- James Chaney, Andrew Goodman, and Michael Schwerner--- who were abducted from their car in Philadelphia, MS by night on a lonely stretch of highway on June 21, 1964. Thoughts like this hovered above Hansell like a dark cloud and kept him from really being free to be himself. He shared his uneasiness with Lonnie who reassured him that everything was going to be okay.

Lonnie kept his concerns to himself. He was quietly reflecting on the fact that George Wallace was now the new governor of Alabama and thinking of how his public stand and comments about race relations might affect any passersby. However, Lonnie refused to let his concerns grip him.

The two made it back to their car and moved it off the road towards a nearby small ravine to keep from being hit by distracted motorists. They settled in for the night to make the best of clearly an uncomfortable situation. Just before dawn, they were awakened by an older white male; his piercing blue  eyes bearing down on them through their window. They immediately noticed that he was driving a pickup truck. But, his eyes and the tone of his raspy voice held their attention. He asked them, "What are y'all doing there?"

Lonnie immediately rolled down his window and said, "Sir, we ran out of gas. We are on our way back to school at Montevallo." Hansell appeared frozen, not saying a word as he was reliving his worst nightmare as a black man being confronted by a white man in a pickup truck in the dark of night. Hansell had played that scenario out over and over in his mind, and the black man never came out alive. He knew he was painting all white people with one negative brush stroke, but his perception was his reality. He was having a hard time escaping the abhorrent imagery to which he had been exposed growing up in Egypt, MS.

The man told Lonnie and Hansell to get out of the car. They heeded his words as they silently opened the car doors and got out. They were both fearful and cautious, and neither made any abrupt moves to suggest that they were not going to be compliant. "Get in the truck" were the next words uttered to them. Lonnie and Hansell remained quiet as the two got into the truck with this stranger, not knowing what was going to happened next.

Their ride for the next few minutes was quiet. No sounds nor words were uttered. The awkward silence was unnerving as Lonnie and Hansell realized that they were not in control of anything. To their surprise, the stranger who never told them his name stopped at the gas station they had passed up the night before which was now open. He allowed them to purchase and put gas in a gas can, and without saying a word, he took the two back to their car.

Lonnie and Hansell got out of the truck and immediately began putting gas into their car. Lonnie's little blue Datsun quickly responded to the fuel. The two student-athletes looked to the white man, the stranger, who asked nothing of them to say, "Thank you." He bowed his head and drove off as they left. The experience significantly impacted Lonnie and Hansell and would cause them to modify their perspectives on race and human relations forever.

Chapter 14
The Unexpected But Welcomed Roommate

Life at the University of Montevallo (UM) often presented new and unusual experiences for the two young men from Mississippi. Despite overcoming challenges on the court, Lonnie and Hansell dealt with even more challenges in the classroom and in the dormitory. Some guests were welcomed while others were evicted, such as the opossum/racoon!

Later in their first year at UM, Lonnie and Hansell had a joint humanistic experience. Secretly, they offered refuge to a white male student, whose last name was also Edwards, as another roommate. This student was not related to Lonnie but stayed with them for a couple of weeks. He had gotten in trouble at home and did not have a place to stay. It seems that one of the best things to happen to him was meeting Lonnie.

Faced with the dilemma of becoming homeless, he sought out Lonnie on campus and shared his plight with him, hoping for some kind of solution. Having a roommate of a different race was a defining moment in the lives of all three. For the first time, Hansell did not see black and white but another person just like him with fears, anxieties, and hopes, just trying to survive.

Lonnie and Hansell made the decision to quietly bring Edwards on board. His luck quickly changed with this move. Lonnie and Hansell were known for having hearty appetites at breakfast, lunch, and dinner. Their meals, which occasionally spilled over into the dorm, increased in size as they bought food back for their new roommate. Their new roomie never knew any hungry days nor lacked a place to sleep with his new brothers. Lonnie and Hansell disassembled their bunk beds, placed them side-by-side, and pushed them together. Their new roommate slept in the middle. This was a far better option than sleeping on the floor. It seems that one of the best things to happen to him was meeting Lonnie.

On a bright sunny day, Lonnie was walking back to his dorm from his archery class when three white female classmates almost passed him in their car. However, when they saw him walking, they stopped and asked if he wanted to ride with them. Lonnie was almost at his dorm, so he hopped in their convertible thinking that they were going to drop him off there. However, to his dismay, instead, the driver kept going and drove through the City of Montevallo. As they were "touring" the city, Lonnie noticed people looking out of store windows and coming out to stand on the front porches of their homes, just staring at them. It WAS an unusual sight at the time! After a short fun ride, the girls dropped Lonnie off safely at his dorm. No incident!

Hansell saw himself growing by leaps and bounds from Egypt, MS. That scared little boy was no longer fearful of white people and what they might do. He began to recognize his own strengths and his compassion for helping others. The positive experience with his white roommate as well as the aid he received from his baseball coaches caused Hansell to reexamine his beliefs. The walls of defense he had so carefully erected to protect himself from the hurt he knew white people could inflict, were slowly lowered. For the first time, Hansell stopped painting all white people with one broad stroke of a brush. He began to see people as individuals and evaluate each one based on their character.

Chapter 15
Scouting and Recruitment Trips

Lonnie and Hansell discovered new support from teammates after the team began winning. On the court, their teammates rallied to support them. Lonnie noticed that when white players on opposing college teams began to get overly physical with him, his teammates would come to his defense. For his teammates, Lonnie's race no longer mattered as he was their Co-Captain and one of their leading scorers. Their team was experiencing something new --- winning. Lonnie couldn't help but inwardly smile when one of his teammates threatened to beat up another white player who he felt was targeting him. How things had changed!

With the team melding as a single unit, Coach Jones began to prepare for the next season. Finding success with both Lonnie and Hansell, he comfortably and enthusiastically recruited other black players. Scouting for new players presented opportunities for Lonnie to go on recruiting trips. He had the luxury of helping to select some of his future teammates. Lonnie was the marquee player with whom black people at the Junior colleges were familiar and were often eager to meet. Coach Jones recognized that he was a good judge of character and skills. He also knew the kind of player that would fit in well at Montevallo. So, it was a successful partnership on the road.

Occasionally, when Lonnie traveled across the State line with Coach Jones, state troopers would pull them over. Lonnie understood the communications protocol of the era. He remained quiet as the coach explained that he was on a recruiting trip and that Lonnie was one of his players. Coach Jones was surprised to find out how well-known and well-liked his marquee player was outside of Montevallo! Since Mississippi was Lonnie's home territory, recruiting there allowed him to travel freely and unencumbered.

Regardless of his new status, Lonnie was still treated with

disdain in most restaurants and hotels after the basketball games ended. He proved, however, that he was able to adapt to any challenges thrown his way. One of his strategies of adaption was being careful about what he ate at certain restaurants!

The recruiting trips often gave Lonnie a chance to test the limits of racial boundaries. He was always skeptical of restaurants that did not serve people like him but only served white people. So, when the basketball team stopped at one of those restaurants to eat, Lonnie always made it a point to order the same meal as the coach. When Coach Jones' meal came first, Lonnie would take the coach's order and begin eating it. While this did not always sit well with Coach Jones, he always had Lonnie's meal sent back for another.

The hotels rarely offered accommodations for Lonnie. Coach Jones compensated for their segregationist position and lack of hospitality to Lonnie by moving him into his room. In his own way, he contributed to tearing down those long-standing walls separating the races. And it also helped on his team's travel budget!

While Lonnie was breaking down racial barriers on his recruiting trips with Coach Jones, Hansell was at the ballpark putting in the work and changing the racial landscape as well. He heard the chants of "Nigger" directed at him dissipating and, instead, heard white people cheering for him. This was a new experience for Hansell, and he welcomed the positive attention. He continued to keep to himself, but clearly, on the inside he was changing. Hansell was becoming more inwardly self-assured, and his newfound confidence was radiating on the outside.

Chapter 16
The Church Splits

Both Lonnie and Hansell began to submerge themselves into the new culture, and each came to appreciate the transition. The students who once shied away from them when they came on campus now approached and engaged them, on friendly terms, in the cafeteria as well as whenever and wherever they saw them on- and off-campus. Even though both "stars" were shining brightly with a modicum of success, the two boys, now men, approached their college fame differently. Hansell chose to take smaller steps; Lonnie was more willing to throw caution to the wind.

So, Langston Hughes asked, "What happens to a dream deferred?" Lonnie would say, "It never goes away. It explodes into a thousand tiny pieces, and it is up to the dreamer to pick up the pieces and carry forward a new dream." Lonnie picked up every fragmented piece and moved towards a purpose driven life.

Lonnie learned that while much progress was being made at the university regarding race relations and acceptance of diversity, the local church was still on the outside looking through its stained-glass windows. Despite all of the spoken goodwill, the local church remained resistant to the changes taking place in the community and on the college campus.

Lonnie and Hansell were invited by some fellow students to attend their local church service at the First Baptist Union Church. Lonnie followed through on the invitation and attended the service that Sunday. While there, he did not notice any overt objection to his presence.

However, to his surprise, back on campus, his white friends who were members of the church informed him that his attendance led to the church splitting. After he visited the church, several members of the congregation left for good. Those who remained continued to reach out to Lonnie and others not previously welcomed in their all-white sanctuary.

Hansell graciously declined the invitation to this church. He had never set foot in a church where white people attended and was not ready for the eyeballing that awaited him. That would have been too much for him to handle. Hansell accepted his celebrity- like recognition and treatment with some trepidation. Attending a white church was a reach for him, and one that he still wasn't ready for yet. Therefore, Hansell attended the local black church in the community on a regular basis. That was where he felt safe.

Even though he had made a lot of progress towards bonding with his white peers and coaches, he was not already to make what he thought was a major change in his religious connections nor in faith-based integration. Hansell approached every new thing with a certain amount of caution, and this was no exception. He remained content to just still be on the periphery of certain aspects of inclusion.

Chapter 17
The Student Teaching Experience and More

Lonnie did his student teaching at Montevallo High School, Montevallo, AL. Except for one situation, his experience was uneventful, following the traditional formula for supplying a teaching experience and training to college students majoring in the field of Education.

During Lonnie's student teaching, a situation arose in which the black students were planning a boycott. The school's student body was predominantly white, but integration had allowed a significant number of black students to enroll. With this diversity came a need for inclusion of students of color in clubs, organizations, and other operations in the school.

The black students raised the issue of there being no black cheerleaders among the cheerleading squad. Seeing no movement by the school's administration toward tackling this issue, they began staging a boycott. The students were supported by their parents and other leaders in the community.

When these plans were brought to Lonnie's attention by some of the students, he became an informal mediator to help both the student leaders, the administration, and community leaders to come to a mutually satisfactory agreement.

After all details were revealed and discussed, the matter was peacefully resolved. Lonnie was commended for his leadership and involvement by the Superintendent of the district, along with many other civic and community leaders. His engagement prevented a serious racial boycott.

At the end of student teaching, just prior to Lonnie's graduation from the University of Montevallo in May of 1971, Mr. Wilburn Adams, Associate Superintendent for the DeKalb County School District, drove over to meet him personally. He wanted to assess Lonnie's qualifications and compatibility for employment in the DeKalb County School District in Decatur, GA.

Mr. Adams' sister was a teacher on the Montevallo High School faculty, and as a result of her developing a favorable view of Lonnie from working with him during his student teaching, encouraged her brother to visit with him. She was extremely impressed with his teaching techniques and the respect he had earned from both faculty and students.

She suggested that Lonnie would be an outstanding candidate for his school district. She further explained that he was a problem-solver and change agent in race relations and could be a real asset to the DeKalb County School District in their challenge with desegregation.

After his visit with Lonnie, Mr. Adams reported back to the Superintendent, Dr. Jim Cherry, that he had found in him a true champion for community and social change. So, Mr. Cherry directed him to invite Lonnie over for a visit.

Since Lonnie was uncertain of where his pursuit of a professional basketball career would lead him, he accepted Mr. Adams' invitation to visit the DeKalb County School District. Visiting the Human Resources Department, he met Mr. Adams again and was introduced to the Director of Personnel, Miss Alice Ann Hamilton, along with members of her staff which included Mrs. Diane Carpenter and Mr. Richard Wark. While there, Lonnie completed the district's employment application and began the interviewing process. At the end of the day, as he left to return to Montevallo to complete his studies for graduation, Lonnie promised to keep in touch.

Chapter 18
College Night Surprise

College Night is a big celebration each year at the University of Montevallo. Activities include a stage play and choosing class favorites. As the process goes, students for each college level class vote on the students selected to represent their class, and the top three finalists (male and female) make speeches at College Night. Afterwards, one male and one female at each college year are selected as "Class Favorites." Final selections are made by a panel of judges.

During Lonnie's senior year, he was selected as one of 10 male students to be voted on to become "Senior Class Favorite." When he found he was nominated, he was surprised, but excited. When the last round of voting had him in the top three finalists, he told Hansell that he was going to prepare his speech and participate in College Night to compete for the title. Hansell tried to discourage him from taking part, telling him that he knew that he was not going to be selected with an all-white panel of judges. Lonnie could not be dissuaded and encouraged Hansell to go to the event with him. Hansell refused and stayed in the dormitory.

Lonnie put on his best and only suit – in brown – and went to College Night. He had written his speech and memorized what he planned to say. When he walked into the event, he noticed that most of the male students had on tuxedos or at least black suits. The female students had on formal gowns. A violinist was playing music in the background. He was the only black student there and the only one in a brown suit. Nevertheless, he kept his composure, summoned his confidence, and interacted with the students as if he was appropriately dressed. Although, it wasn't formal attire, he was still "clean!"

When it was time to make speeches, each nominee came before the students and faculty members in attendance alone while his/her competitors remained sequestered off-stage, unable to hear what the speaker was saying. It finally came time for Lonnie to make his speech. He was escorted to the stage and took his position. As he surveyed the audience, he saw his Speech teacher's face, looking at him with anticipation. So, remembering points from that class --- how to stand, where to look, how to deliver a message, etc. --- he began his speech.

Lonnie told about his background and his journey to get to the University of Montevallo. He told about his positive experiences there and how much he had learned about race relations, human relations, and getting along with people who were different. Lonnie said that he was honored to be a student at "this outstanding university." He then quoted segments of the poem *The Road Not Traveled* by Robert Frost. He told the audience that he too had taken a road less traveled by, in spite of his mother's and his aunt's fears, he had stayed on the road and was scheduled to graduate in May. He told them that he had learned that human relations far exceeded race relations. Lonnie said that he would go on telling the story ages and ages hence that he took the road less traveled and that made a difference in his life. He ended his remarks by saying, "Thanks and good luck as you consider me as the senior class favorite choice." By the end of his speech, many in the audience had tears in their eyes and all gave him a standing ovation.

When he returned to the holding room with his competitors, they heard the applause and cheers in the auditorium and asked him what he said. He told them, "Good luck boys! You're on your own!"

University of Montevallo – 1971
Senior Class Favorites

At the end of the night, the moderators of the program announced the winners of the class favorites beginning with the freshman class. Lonnie noticed that a male student would give flowers to the female class favorite and that a female student would pin a boutonniere on the male class favorite and give him a kiss. When it was time for the Senior Class Favorites, the female student was announced. Then, the announcer said, "and our male Senior Class Favorite is ...." with a noticeable pause, "Lonnie Edwards!" The place erupted with applause! Lonnie broke out into a cold sweat knowing what came next. When the female student was pinning the boutonniere on him, through a smile with clenched teeth, he told her, "Don't kiss me! Don't kiss me!" He was thinking of the racial views at the time. She looked surprised but didn't kiss him. Lonnie took a deep sigh of relief.

When the event ended, he ran all the way back to his dorm to tell Hansell of his selection as the male "Senior Class Favorite." Hansell couldn't believe it. But they celebrated together, reflecting on their experiences there at the college, and saying that maybe a change (in society) had started to come.

Chapter 19
The Thrill of Victory; The Agony of Defeat

It finally happened. Both basketball and baseball seasons had come full circle. Lonnie and Hansell found that their time at the University of Montevallo had come and gone. The integration experiment was a glowing success as Lonnie and Hansell were now flying the coop and making their way out into the grownup world beyond the gates of the University of Montevallo. Their time spent at Montevallo had become meaningful and rewarding as the doors to the university now swung wide open to students of color.

FALCON TROPHY WINNERS - - University of Montevallo athletes receiving special awards at the annual All-Sports Banquet are congratulated by Cliff Harper (right), assistant to the Southeastern Conference Commissioner. Named for special honors were: (from left), James Tuck, McCalla, Dean's Trophy; Lonnie Edwards, Shaw, Miss., Circle K Sportsmanship Trophy and Spirit of '70 Award; and James Hobbs, Athens, Top Rebounder Award and Neal Shirley Award. Harper was guest speaker at the banquet.

Lonnie and Hansell were instrumental in giving the University of Montevallo the first of two winning basketball seasons and with it, more collegiate pride. During this same time, they gained enhanced life skills, a high-quality education, and the expertise and confidence necessary to handle challenges they would face later in life.

The two Coahoma graduates found answers to their burning questions, "Can we coexist with white people?" and "Can we successfully compete both academically and athletically with white people?" The answers to both questions came back as a resounding "Yes, we can!"

Lonnie and Hansell went to Montevallo as black strangers on the campus among a sea of white students and adults. However, in the process, each built life-long friendships and relationships. Both formed irrevocable bonds with their new extended family and community and became a part of something bigger than themselves.

The weekend before graduation, Lonnie was invited by the Head Coach of the Memphis Pros American Basketball Association (ABA) team, "Babe" McCarthy, to travel to Memphis, Tennessee for a workout. Lonnie had an impressive performance. But the ABA Organization was confronting possible closing and going out of business because of financial conditions. So, this opportunity was not a viable one.

Lonnie returned to the university campus, looking forward to participating in the graduation ceremony. Graduating on time and with honors, Lonnie and Hansell had their families in tow, on campus for the first time for this historic event. This was their siblings' first college graduation. It was extremely exciting and inspirational to all of them. The diplomas each received that day were certified and signed by George Wallace, Governor of Alabama. Yes, the same George Wallace, the self-proclaimed segregationist, who blocked the doors at the University of Alabama while activating the Alabama National guard to deny black students Vivien

Malone and James Hood entry; the same man who vowed segregation today, segregation tomorrow, segregation forever!

After graduation, each hugged and waved as they took their separate roads. Lonnie left the University of Montevallo hoping to fulfill his dream of playing basketball in the National Basketball Association (NBA), alongside his heroes Wilt Chamberlain and Bill Russell. Hansell went further south to pursue a career as an educator.

Armed with his McEvans High School jumper that led him out of the cotton field, Lonnie was now ready to take on the tryouts in the Windy City with the Chicago Bulls. But, first, he had to answer a call from the military.

"For more than 50 years, Selective Service and the registration requirement for America's young men have served as a backup system to provide manpower to the U.S. Armed Forces.

President Franklin Roosevelt signed the Selective Training and Service Act of 1940 which created the country's first peacetime draft and formally established the Selective Service System as an independent Federal agency.

From 1948 until 1973, during both peacetime and periods of conflict, men were drafted to fill vacancies in the armed forces which could not be filled through voluntary means. From 1969 - 1973, the U. S. military was drafting men to serve in the Vietnam War. In 1973, the draft ended, and the U.S. converted to an All-Volunteer military.

The registration requirement was suspended in April 1975. It was resumed again in 1980 by President Carter in response to the Soviet invasion of Afghanistan. Registration continues today as a hedge against underestimating the number of servicemen needed in a future crisis. The obligation of a man to register is imposed by the Military Selective Service Act.

The Act establishes and governs the operations of the Selective Service System."
(Source: Selective Service System - June 25, 2001, revision)

Photo: Selective Service System

"December 1, 1969, marked the date of the first draft lottery held since 1942. This drawing determined the order of induction for men born between January 1, 1944, and December 31, 1950. A large glass container held 366 blue plastic balls containing every possible birth date and affecting men between 18 and 26 years old.

Upon receiving official notice of the lottery's results, local draft boards will arrange their files of registrants accordingly and draft in the order dates were drawn. Following the drawing of dates, including Feb. 29 for men born in a leap year, the 26 letters of the alphabet were drawn to determine the order for induction for men registered with the same draft board and having the same birthday. After a board has filled its draft quota for the year, those men whose birthdays have not been reached will be free of all draft liability except in time of extreme national emergency.

As a general rule, Selective Service expects those with dates drawn in the upper third of the list will be drafted. Those in the middle third are of questionable status and those in the bottom third will not have to serve." (Source: https://15thfar.org/draft.html)

ORDER TO REPORT FOR PHYSICAL EXAM

SELECTIVE SERVICE SYSTEM   Approval Not Required.

ORDER TO REPORT FOR
ARMED FORCES PHYSICAL EXAMINATION

LOCAL BOARD NO. 8
FEDERAL BUILDING
1000 LIBERTY AVE.
PITTSBURGH PA. 15282

(Local Board Stamp)
FEB 6 1970
(Date of mailing)

SELECTIVE SERVICE NO.
36 | 8 | 50 | 685

To
JOHN DOE
123 MAIN ST.
ANY TOWN, PA 15222

You are hereby directed to present yourself for Armed Forces Physical Examination by reporting at:

ASSEMBLY ROOM - 17th FLOOR FEDERAL BLDG.
1000 LIBERTY AVENUE
(Place of reporting)

on FEB 18 1970 at 7 A.M.
(Date)   (Hour)

M. F. Gallo
(Member Executive Secretary or clerk of Local Board)

IMPORTANT NOTICE
(Read Each Paragraph Carefully)

TO ALL REGISTRANTS:
When you report pursuant to this order you will be forwarded to an Armed Forces Examining Station where it will be determined whether you are qualified for military service under current standards...

TO CLASS I-A AND I-A-O REGISTRANTS:
If you fail to report for examination as directed, you may be declared delinquent...

TO CLASS I-O REGISTRANTS:
This examination is given for the purpose of determining whether you are qualified for military service...

SSS Form 223 (Revised 9-29-65)

This letter was the first step of being "drafted" into the armed services.

ORDER TO REPORT FOR INDUCTION

SELECTIVE SERVICE SYSTEM

Approval Not Required.

ORDER TO REPORT FOR INDUCTION

The President of the United States,

To

JOHN DOE
123 MAIN ST.
ANY TOWN, PA 15222

LOCAL BOARD NO. 8
FEDERAL BUILDING
1000 LIBERTY AVE.
PITTSBURGH, PA. 15222
(Local Board Stamp)

APR 23 1970
(Date of mailing)

SELECTIVE SERVICE NO.

| 36 | 8 | 50 | 665 |

GREETING:

You are hereby ordered for induction into the Armed Forces of the United States, and to report

at ASSEMBLY ROOM - 17th FLOOR, FEDERAL BLDG
1000 LIBERTY AVENUE, PITTSBURGH, PA.
(Place of reporting)

on **MAY 20 1970** at **7 A.M.**
(Date) (Hour)

for forwarding to an Armed Forces Induction Station.

(Member, Executive Secretary, or Clerk of Local Board)

IMPORTANT NOTICE
(Read Each Paragraph Carefully)

If you are so far from your own local board that reporting in compliance with this Order will be a serious hardship, go immediately to any local board and make written request for transfer of your delivery for induction, taking this Order with you.

IF YOU HAVE HAD PREVIOUS MILITARY SERVICE, OR ARE NOW A MEMBER OF THE NATIONAL GUARD OR A RESERVE COMPONENT OF THE ARMED FORCES, BRING EVIDENCE WITH YOU. IF YOU WEAR GLASSES, BRING THEM. IF MARRIED, BRING PROOF OF YOUR MARRIAGE. IF YOU HAVE ANY PHYSICAL OR MENTAL CONDITION WHICH, IN YOUR OPINION, MAY DISQUALIFY YOU FOR SERVICE IN THE ARMED FORCES, BRING A PHYSICIAN'S CERTIFICATE DESCRIBING THAT CONDITION, IF NOT ALREADY FURNISHED TO YOUR LOCAL BOARD.

Valid documents are required to substantiate dependency claims in order to receive basic allowance for quarters. Be sure to take the following with you when reporting to the induction station. The documents will be returned to you. (a) FOR LAWFUL WIFE OR LEGITIMATE CHILD UNDER 21 YEARS OF AGE—original, certified copy or photostat of a certified copy of marriage certificate, child's birth certificate, or a public or church record of marriage issued over the signature and seal of the custodian of the church or public records; (b) FOR LEGALLY ADOPTED CHILD—certified court order of adoption; (c) FOR CHILD OF DIVORCED SERVICE MEMBER (Child in custody of person other than claimant)—(1) Certified or photostatic copies of receipts from custodian of child evidencing serviceman's contributions for support and (2) Divorce decree, court support order or separation order; (d) FOR DEPENDENT PARENT affidavits establishing that dependency.

Bring your Social Security Account Number Card. If you do not have one, apply at nearest Social Security Administration Office. If you have life insurance, bring a record of the insurance company's address and your policy number. Bring enough clean clothes for 3 days. Bring enough money to last 1 month for personal purchases.

This Local Board will furnish transportation and meals and lodging when necessary, from the place of reporting to the induction station where you will be examined. If found qualified you will be inducted into the Armed Forces. If found not qualified, return transportation and meals and lodging when necessary, will be furnished to the place of reporting.

You may be found not qualified for induction. Keep this in mind in arranging your affairs, to prevent any undue hardship if you are not inducted. If employed, inform your employer of this possibility. Your employer can then be prepared to continue your employment if you are not inducted. To protect your right to return to your job if you are not inducted, you must report for work as soon as possible after the completion of your induction examination. You may jeopardize your reemployment rights if you do not report for work at the beginning of your next regularly scheduled working period after you have returned to your place of employment.

Willful failure to report at the place and hour of the day named in this Order subjects the violator to fine and imprisonment. Bring this Order with you when you report.

SSS Form 252 (Revised 4-29-63) (Further printings may be used until exhausted.)

This letter meant you were "drafted" into the armed services

The following news article appeared in newspapers the day after the 1969 draft lottery; December 2, 1969

* * * * *

Sept. 14 'Wins' Draft Lottery
June 8 Brings Up The Rear; 850,000 Affected by Drawing

By Mike Miller (Excerpts from article)

WASHINGTON -- The Selective Service System today was notifying the nation's 4,000 draft boards to arrange their files of draft eligible young men for 1970 with those born Sept. 14 at the top of the heap to be called up first. And the official notice sent to state and local Selective Service authorities places those men with June 8 birthdays in 366th position -- at the very bottom.

That was the start and the finish of last night's long-awaited lottery-by-birthday drawing, which opened with an invocation and closed with a benediction. In between, it saw the draft future being determined for an estimated 850,000 young men, many of whom must have been saying their own prayers about the results.

For those with birthdays drawn in the upper portion of the lottery list -- April 24, Dec. 30, Feb. 14, Oct. 18, Sept. 6, Oct. 26, Sept. 7, Nov. 22 and Dec. 6 round out the top 10 -- the uncertainty over their draft status has ended.

They now know they will be drafted early in the year unless they volunteer first. And those at the bottom know that they will not be drafted and can plan their lives accordingly. For those in the middle or marginal area of the drawing, uncertainty still exists. But they certainly will know definitely by the end of 1970 whether they will be inducted.

The lottery was conducted in low key fashion with young men and women representing Selective Service's youth advisory committees in the various states drawing capsules containing slips of paper with the birth dates on them from a water-cooler size glass bowl.

Rep. Alexander Pirnie, New York Republican who drew the first date, was the only person in an official capacity to pull out the capsule. About a dozen youthful demonstrators picketed outside, denouncing the draft, the lottery and the Vietnam war, but they failed to interfere with the smooth precision of the drawing.

Following the drawing of dates, including Feb. 29 for men born in a leap year, the young people also drew the 26 letters of the alphabet to determine the order for induction for men registered with the same draft board and having the same birthday. J was drawn first, V last. Thus, a man named Jones would be drafted before Vickery under those circumstances.

Upon receiving official notice of the lottery's results, local draft boards will arrange their files of registrants accordingly and draft in the order dates were drawn. After a board has filled its draft quota for the year, those men whose birthdays have not been reached will be free of all draft liability except in time of extreme national emergency.

As a general rule, Selective Service expects those with dates drawn in the upper third of the list will be drafted. Those in the middle third are of questionable status and those in the bottom third will not have serve.

The estimated 850,000 who will be 19 through 25 and classified 1-A or draft eligible as of Jan. 1 are directly affected by last night's drawing. After the first year, only men 19 at the beginning of the year and older men with deferments which have expired will be affected by the annual lotteries. For men now in the 19-25 pool with college or other deferments, the position their birthdays were drawn will determine their liability in the year their deferments expire.

Leading up to his college graduation, Lonnie's excitement was building in anticipation of his having an opportunity to play in the NBA. On one day, he was notified of his graduation status; the next day, he received a letter from the Chicago Bulls, inviting him to their Rookie Camp in Chicago, IL. Then, the next day, Lonnie received an ORDER TO REPORT FOR PHYSICAL EXAM for the U. S. Military.

In the 1969 Lottery, out of 366 numbers, Lonnie's birthday was assigned the number #51; Hansell's birthday was assigned the number #350. As a result, being drafted appeared to be imminent in Lonnie's future, but not in Hansell's.

So, with much anxiety, Lonnie followed the military's instructions to report to Calera, AL. (about seven miles west of Montevallo) There, he would travel with other potential recruits on a bus going to Montgomery, AL to take his physical at Maxwell Gunter Air Force Base.

When boarding the bus for Montgomery, Lonnie noticed that one of the men in his group was given an envelope. No explanation was provided to the entire group about the envelope, so he thought that the man possessing it was special in some way.

Arriving at the base in Montgomery, Lonnie and the group of men with whom he traveled were directed to an area to sit and wait until they were called to begin taking their physicals.

Lonnie expected that they would be finished by 2:00 p.m. in the afternoon. Then, they would reboard the bus to return to Calera. That would give him time to get to the Chicago Bulls' Rookie Camp which started on the next day.

Sitting and waiting, Lonnie noticed men being called in groups by their originating cities to begin their physicals as well as others leaving after theirs were completed. Time went by ... 9:00 a.m. ... 10:00 a.m. ...11:00 a.m. ... and Lonnie's group was not being called. During this waiting period, there were no cell phones, iPads, electronic tablets, etc. to keep them occupied. Conversation was minimal. The TV monitors only had military information on them. So, it was a long, dismal, anxiety-filled wait.

Finally, about 4:00 p.m., when Lonnie's group had not been called, he went over to the man holding the envelope and asked him if he knew what was in the envelope. When he responded that he did not, Lonnie asked him to give the envelope to the officer who was in charge for the day. When the officer opened the envelope, he spoke to the potential recruit in an aggravated, rough voice, "You've been sitting here all day and are just now giving me this envelope?" After the potential recruit said, "Yes," the officer said, "Then, your group will stay overnight and begin your physicals in the morning!"

Not only was the officer upset, but so was Lonnie! This change in their schedule was going to make him late for joining the Bulls Camp.

When Lonnie's group arrived at their designated barracks, he noticed men jumping directly into beds, but he also noticed strong body odors that were going to make spending the night in close quarters almost unbearable. So, he took charge saying, "Everybody has to get in the shower before bed! Get up and get going!" Surprisingly, no one challenged Lonnie's assuming this level of control. Everybody hit the showers!

The next morning, Lonnie's group was awakened by 6:00 a.m. and was told to report for breakfast at 7:00 a.m. They began their physicals at 9:00 a.m., finished them by 2:00 p.m., and immediately boarded the bus to return to Calera, AL. Needless to say, Lonnie passed the physical and was classified 1-A or "draft eligible."

Upon arriving in Calera, AL, Lonnie jumped into his car and drove nearly 350 miles to his aunt's and uncle's house in his hometown of Shaw, MS, arriving about midnight. While driving, his underlying fear of flying weighed heavily on his mind. Lonnie's only airline flight had been from Daytona Beach, FL to Birmingham, AL. It was gifted to him by his close friend Earnest Killum, then a second-round draft choice with the Los Angeles Lakers. As one might imagine, flying into Chicago was expected to be much more challenging. Adding to this challenge was having to navigate his way from O'Hare Airport, one of the world's largest and busiest, to DePaul University where the Bull's camp was being held. But Lonnie was ready to tackle this challenge. After a long day, feeling exhausted but excited, Lonnie fell asleep with dreams of being an NBA star on his mind.

The next day, Lonnie's excitement grew as his Aunt Bertha and Uncle James Rodges drove him 140 miles to the airport in Memphis, TN to board a plane for Chicago, IL.

Arriving in Chicago, things worked out. Lonnie made it safely to DePaul University and joined the three-day Chicago Bulls Rookie basketball camp on Day 2. Surveying the groups of men playing basketball or waiting their turns to play, he saw that there were more than a hundred candidates vying to fill one (1) position being vacated by retiring point guard Bobby Wise. Upon his entering the gym, a trainer took Lonnie over to be introduced to the Bull's Head Coach, Dick Motta, along with basketball player Jerry Sloan who was helping in the camp. When Lonnie explained his delay was due to the military physical, he was allowed to join the camp in progress.

Lonnie arrived at the camp in "tip-top" condition. As a result, during the tryouts, he was fierce as his offensive and defensive prowess were both up to par, NBA caliber. The Bulls were impressed with his performance. The elimination process was rough for the one hundred or so eager, potential NBA players, but Lonnie was kept through cut after cut. Sometimes, he was the only player retained in a group when assessments were made on who to keep and who to let go.

At the end of the camp, Lonnie was chosen to be one of the final ten rookie players considered for the open point guard position. However, when the final decision was announced, he was released. Norm Van Lier was selected instead. In the end, it was Lonnie's low U. S. military draft lottery number for the Vietnam War that was the deciding factor in the choice.

The military won. With a lottery number 51 and a classification of 1-A, Lonnie was on target for the military draft. The Bulls leadership expressed regret that they could not offer him a permanent slot on the team because of his draft status, wished him well, and let him go.

Lonnie was crushed, and he felt lost. He sought solace in his efforts to respond to the question Langston Hughes asked, "What happens to a dream deferred?" Lonnie was now on a painful quest to find his own answer. All he could think was, "… a change is gonna come!"

Although Lonnie left the Chicago Bulls' tryouts heartbroken, he continued to work out playing basketball on the street courts and the local gyms. He bided his time living with his father and working in a factory in Chicago, fully expecting that when his November birthday came, he would have to report for duty in the U.S. military.

Chapter 20
Defeat Does Not Last Forever

During the time he was working in Chicago, waiting to be drafted, Lonnie received a call from his Aunt Bertha Rodges telling him that a representative from the DeKalb County School District (DCSD) in Decatur, Georgia (about 20 miles east of Atlanta) had been looking for him. DCSD representatives had met Lonnie on the campus of the University of Montevallo while they were recruiting teachers. They knew he was an Education major and had a teaching assignment to offer him.

Aunt Bertha provided Lonnie with the telephone number to return the call to Richard Wark, Personnel Administrator with DCSD. Mr. Wark was impressed with how Lonnie had navigated the college culture and felt he would be a great fit for the DeKalb school district which was under a court-ordered desegregation plan. During their conversation, Mr. Wark offered Lonnie a teaching position. Lonnie told him about his draft status – being #51 in the draft, yet Mr. Wark insisted on offering him employment. Mr. Wark told him that they would handle his draft situation when the time came.

Although Lonnie was uncertain where it would lead or even how long it would last, he accepted the job. So, he took the long train ride back from Illinois to Mississippi and picked up his uncle's, Big Cuz/Coach Rodges', little blue Datsun to drive to Georgia. Lonnie felt that he had finally found his ram in the bush and was charting a new course while keeping open his other options!

Lonnie began the Fall 1971 school year teaching at Hooper-Alexander Elementary School. However, as expected, he was drafted on November 5, 1971, and was directed to report to be inducted into the military on December 8, 1971.
When he shared this information with Mr. Wark, the DeKalb County School Board of Education requested from the

Selective Service that Lonnie would be granted a deferment, supplying them time to find a suitable replacement. The deferment was granted and during the period of his deferment, the Military Draft became all-volunteer. As a result, he was able to continue teaching, and after reflecting on the many obstacles he had overcome, he was sure that his mission and purpose was to be fulfilled in the DeKalb County School District. Lonnie felt that he was now taking a page from his favorite Robert Frost poem, 'The Road Not Taken,' to become a bridge that would open segregated roads everywhere, allowing others to freely cross over to the other side.

Chapter 21
Sweet Home Alabama

Hansell not only graduated with honors, but he also left the University of Montevallo being named among the Falcons' outstanding student-athletes and scholars. His time at Montevallo was a coming-of-age period for him. Many times, he reflected upon the man he was now becoming.

Hansell was no longer intimidated by or in awe of white people. In fact, the experience had moved him to a new comfort zone. U. S. President Franklin D. Roosevelt's (FDR) inaugural quote, "the only thing we have to fear is fear itself," was a true philosophy. He had found his niche! He went to Montevallo unsure and unproven, in many ways, but left the campus confident and self-assured, as a result of his status as one of two black male student-athletes who not only survived but thrived in a sea of whiteness.

As previously mentioned, Lonnie accepted a job in metro Atlanta, Georgia, a growing metropolis, attracting individuals from many communities of color. However, to the surprise of Hansell's family, he chose to take his newfound confidence and remain in Alabama, continuing to live in a predominately white world. They expected him to go to a northern U. S. state or pursue a position leading him back to the black community. He accepted a job in Vestavia, AL, some thirty miles north of Montevallo. In this town, the population was approximately 90 percent Caucasian. However, this time. Hansell arrived with more survival tools than he took to Montevallo.

Unlike Lonnie who left Montevallo to pursue an NBA career, Hansell did not carry the same passion for playing basketball. He envisioned instead, a career among the professional ranks in the field of Education. This was a vision that he had kept hidden deep within and had not shared with anyone, not even with his roommate. His time at Montevallo helped him broaden his aspirations. Vestavia offered an opportunity for Hansell to reinvent himself by exploring his options and testing unchartered waters. He now stepped into a new role in Alabama getting what he wanted the first time out. He was hired to be a Physical Education (PE) teacher and coach at Vestavia Junior High School, the same place where he did his student teaching.

Coaching was a new opportunity and experience for Hansell, although he had thought about it while at the University. He was especially mindful of the private sessions his baseball coaches provided him after practice, teaching him the correct signs and signals. Hansell learned from the best at both Coahoma and Montevallo! He was determined that the training and techniques he missed as a child would not be missed by his students and players. So, right away, he started sharing and implementing the things he learned.

Settling down in Vestavia, AL, Hansell brought with him a swagger that comes with being a University of Montevallo alumnus. He was brimming with the self-assuredness and confidence that he did not have when he arrived at Montevallo. Hansell was now tested, proven, and ready for the challenge. He was a winner, and this time, he believed it!

When Hansell walked into Vestavia Junior High School, he felt right at home. The ice had already been broken with his tenure at Montevallo. It no longer mattered that he was the only black person on the staff. He saw the world through a different set of lenses. Hansell now had a new beginning, and he was eagerly looking forward to all the possibilities.

In Alabama, "Mr. Gunn" found that working at Vestavia Junior High School was an amazing experience. He knew that he was in the first quarter of his career, and oh boy, what a first quarter he was having! In high school, Hansell was a scoring machine. His skillfulness continued at Coahoma Junior College as well as at the University of Montevallo. Now, his performance in his roles as a teacher and as a coach at Vestavia felt like he was in control of the basketball again. His success in the classroom with his white students carried over to his coaching.

His students greatly benefited from his collegiate basketball experience by his exposing them to college level coaching. Hansell was now changing the sports landscape and creating a winning culture.

Prior to his arrival, this predominately white school had no winning history. Now, his boys looked forward to practice as well as his camps for added training. In between those times, Hansell participated in pickup basketball games with his some of his students in the neighborhood, and they saw firsthand that he not only "talked the talk, but he walked the walk" as well. They knew he was the "real deal." His style of coaching gave him, and them, the edge they needed over the competition.

Hansell's first year as a teacher and coach at Vestavia proved successful. He coached both his eighth-grade boys' basketball and baseball teams to county championships. That following year, he quickly proved that it was not a fluke. This rookie phenom gave a repeat performance the next year with his boys' basketball team winning the county championship again. Hansell wasn't dreaming; he was wide awake and enjoying every minute of the ride!

Chapter 22
New Mountains to Climb

Lonnie J. Edwards,
First-year teacher

In the fall of 1971, Lonnie's journey into the DeKalb County School District (DCSD) was far different than the jubilant celebration ushering him on to the University of Montevallo's basketball court chanting, "We want Lonnie! We want Lonnie!" He was hired by DCSD when schools all over our nation were being forced to integrate. At the time, the DeKalb school system was the largest in the State of Georgia with more than 100,000 students and over 10,000 employees.

"Litigation in DeKalb County, Georgia, over school desegregation began in 1968 with the filing of a class action lawsuit (Pitts v. Cherry) against the DeKalb County Board of Education to end the practice of racial segregation. In 1969, the U.S. District Court for the Northern District of Georgia imposed a desegregation plan upon the DeKalb school system and retained authority to oversee the implementation of the plan. The plan had three stages of implementation. In the first stage (1969-1972), the District Court made the ruling that DeKalb County Schools must desegregate, as required by Brown v. Board of Education, and the school system went to work on the plan. The school system had the financial ability to close all of the black schools, so they did not have the challenge of resistance from white families who did not want to have their children at historically black schools.

These schools were as follows:
- Victoria Simmons Elementary, Stone Mountain
- Robert Shaw Elementary, Scottdale
- County Line Elementary, Ellenwood

- Lynwood Park Elementary and High School, Chamblee
- Hamilton High School, Scottdale
- Bruce Street High School, Lithonia

With the black schools closed, DeKalb Schools' leadership reset the attendance boundaries, and it seemed like their work was done. But it was not!

The criteria for integration included student assignments, transportation, physical facilities, extracurricular activities, faculty assignments, and resource allocations.

In 1989, a court decision found that not all of the criteria were met and required the school board to remain under complete court supervision until full integration was achieved.

After many years of litigation, the case went to the U.S. Supreme Court in 1992 at which point it was the longest running case in Georgia's history. After a few more years of litigation resulting from the Supreme Court ruling, the case was closed in 1997. The DeKalb County School System was declared integrated, and therefore the school board no longer required judicial supervision."

Source: rbrl.blogspot.com/2016/09/school-desegregation-in-dekalb-county.html
Post by Adriane Hanson, Digital Curation and Processing Archivist

The experience and skills gained at the University of Montevallo in Alabama paid great dividends early on as Lonnie transitioned into his new career as a Physical Education, Reading, and Science teacher. He took his talents to Metro Atlanta, Georgia and made a commitment to change the landscape of human relations one student, one parent, one administrator, and one community leader at a time. The DeKalb County School District now had a bona-fide experienced change agent who was now committing to come aboard and create a win, win environment.

Lonnie immediately identified a lack of effective and open communication among administrators, staff, parents, and community leaders. However, his UM experience had helped him to develop skills to improve communication and to foster inclusion. So, he went to work not only to instruct children, but to improve the school and community climate.

Expecting to quickly build bridges for others to cross, Lonnie planned to arm them with proven, effective, hands-on learning and community-based activities. He was ready to use his skills to stimulate learners' interest and increase participation at both the student and parent levels, leaving them begging for more.

But, before Lonnie could walk into a classroom, he had to pass a specific test. That meant that he had to get past Mrs. Narvie J. Harris, a seasoned black female, considered an education guru and affectionally known as "the Black Superintendent." Mrs. Harris was an unofficial educational coordinator who made sure black people who were hired, were well-equipped to teach in the all-black schools. Somehow, Lonnie managed to get hired before meeting her.

Steen Miles, Lonnie Edwards, & Narvie Harris

However, shortly after he was hired, Lonnie met Mrs. Harris as he left out of the Personnel Office in the school district's Central Administration building. Startled to see him, she asked who he was since prior to then, she knew all black people hired by the district. After finding out that he was a new teacher she had not sanctioned, she still asked to see his lesson plans. Lonnie was taken aback as he had none.

Actually, he was preoccupied with finding somewhere to live so that he could stop sleeping in his car. Realizing that he had no lesson plans, Mrs. Harris took Lonnie under her wings, spent the afternoon with him, and helped write his lesson plans. In reality, Mrs. Harris did most of the writing. So, before she turned him loose, Lonnie's lesson plans were solid and ready for him to show the white principal, at the predominantly white school, that he would be meeting the next day. As they parted, Mrs. Harris told Lonnie that if he needed anything else to call on her. He expressed his appreciation and left to look for permanent housing.

The next day, Lonnie reported to his new school, Hooper Alexander Elementary, and met with the principal who, clearly, was not looking forward to having him there. There were four black female teachers on the staff; Lonnie was the first and only black male teacher. The setting felt familiar to him, like Montevallo, but smaller.

The principal avoided eye contact with Lonnie, looking down and away while talking with him. After a little small talk, the principal quickly asked to see his lesson plans. To his surprise, Lonnie was ready. His chance meeting with Mrs. Harris had prepared him for this moment!

Perusing his lesson plans, the principal asked Lonnie about his plan to teach square dancing. Lonnie was able to relate his experience learning and teaching it on Montevallo's campus. Afterwards, he left the principal's office knowing there would be some challenges, but nothing that he couldn't overcome … or so he thought.

As the school year moved on, Lonnie found himself getting acclimated in his new surrounding but also thinking about his missed NBA career as well as his friend who was playing professional basketball. In November of 1971, the Los Angeles Lakers of the NBA were on a 16-0 winning streak on the road, dominating all opponents. Lonnie had been a Laker fan for years, and his interest in them increased when, in 1970, they drafted his junior college teammate and best friend, Earnest Killum, after a successful college career at Stetson University in Florida.

For a few minutes in his busy day, Lonnie's mind drifted, reflecting on his dream of facing Killum as a star on the Chicago Bulls roster that year. However, that was now a dream deferred or maybe even cancelled as Lonnie had embarked on a new career path. Nevertheless, he still kept up with Earnie's press clippings and secretly thought that he too might someday play for the NBA.

(Note: Years later the DeKalb County School System named a Theme School in honor of Mrs. Narvie J. Harris.)

Lonnie leading children in activity in classroom

Chapter 23
A Secret Exposed

The brightly colored leaves falling from the trees in Georgia signaled the Fall season was at hand. Because of the cooler weather, Lonnie was forced to provide instruction for his gym classes inside a large, combined classroom. He prepared his fifth-grade students for square dancing, but he was in for a rude awakening! Little did Lonnie know that a tiny, petite, frail, blond girl returning to Hooper this school year was going to change his life, giving it a renewed purpose.

In school, this little girl, Nancy Johnson, was practically invisible, by choice. She was adept at seeming to vanish in a room, like a chameleon in a forest, keeping a secret that made her a recluse and friendless. At Hooper Alexander, Nancy was one of the forty- five children in a typical classroom and was not openly clamoring for attention. She chose to be the Shrinking Violet.

Nancy Johnson

At school, Nancy wore a facade, hiding something that only felt natural at home. The other children weren't kind towards her; not that she cared as she kept to herself. She was guarded and without a single friend. This ten-year-old was living a double life. At home, Nancy was the oldest of her two siblings, and was the most active and engaging. But, at school, she was a shy introvert.

Nancy's family moved to Georgia from Florida in the middle of the previous year. Apparently, she had some challenges at her old school and was determined to prevent those challenges from happening at the new school. Being cautious with others,

Nancy didn't bond with any of her peers or her teachers. Most of her teachers walked past her desk and sat at their desks in the back of their classrooms without even stopping to engage her in conversation. She was used to getting overlooked in school, like last year in her old school (before she came to Hooper), and did not expect that this year and this school would be any different.

However, things at Hooper did change when Nancy had an up-close encounter with the new, 6' tall, black gym teacher --- "Mr. Edwards." This was Mr. Edwards' first year at Hooper Alexander Elementary School. So, he was just "getting his feet wet" in the classroom. Mr. Edwards was a rookie, a novice to the classroom, and an unwanted addition to a teaching staff that was reluctant to share with him critical pieces of information relative to any of his students.

All that Nancy saw when she looked at Mr. Edwards was a giant of a man. Whenever he was near, she found herself looking up as he cast a shadow over her like a big oak shade tree. It didn't matter to Nancy that he was her first black male teacher and that almost everyone else was white. Mr. Edwards was popular with the kids, well-dressed, and had style.

Nancy had met other black men before, but not at school. They were usually coming around to the back door of her home to see her father. Her dad preferred it that way, albeit much to the disapproval of her mom. Nancy's mother was a nurse and had treated many sick or injured patients, black and white. In fact, at one time, she worked at a hospital in Selma, Alabama and provided medical treatment for black people who were injured marching across the Edmund Pettus Bridge for voters' rights. Nancy was proud of her mom because she kept it real. Nancy thought, "People are people." She believed that her dad's bigotry was nonsense and not to be modeled.

However, unexpectedly, something happened that school year to give Nancy's dad an attitude adjustment about black people. He was involved in a serious car accident, and five black men present at the scene rescued him from his mangled car. He was confused as to what caused the accident, but he was even more confused as to why the black men pulled him out of the car, saving his life. When he asked them why they had helped him, they told him that he was a human being and that his life mattered.

Reflecting on their behaviors and responses, Nancy's father became ashamed of his past racist thoughts and behaviors. He began to make amends, grateful for being alive and for having a new opportunity to start building positive relationships with black people and other people of color.

Mr. Edwards was a personable teacher who, despite his overcrowded classroom, went out of his way to connect with his students, even though Nancy made it a point to appear disinterested. The students had Mr. Edwards for gym, science, and reading, but most looked forward to gym because he was the only teacher they had for play time. When Mr. Edwards changed from his suit and tie into his gym outfit for play time, the kids regarded him as one of them.

He was different than other teachers, and the children noticed it right away. They valued the time he spent with them; he made learning fun, and he was a good listener. Kids felt that they could talk to Mr. Edwards, although Nancy wasn't one of them. Instead, she chose to be a casual observer in class, bound not to let him or anyone at school get close to her, for she had a secret that she would protect, no matter the cost.

Nancy noticed that Mr. Edwards' life at Hooper Alexander wasn't so easy either. His popularity with the students did not transfer early on to the mostly white female teachers on staff. When Mr. Edwards' students lined up in the hallway to go to lunch or to the bathroom, white female teachers passing by him would not extend cordial greetings. Instead, they chose to avoid making eye contact with him by looking at the wall or ceiling. Mr. Edwards appeared amused by their behavior as it was like the behavior he experienced with both teachers and students while attending the University of Montevallo. At Montevallo, he would turn the tables by beating them to look away at the wall and ceiling first. At Hooper, when his students saw Mr. Edwards look away, as if to snub other teachers, they tried to smother their grins.

Every day, Mr. Edwards led several sessions of physical education classes for 30 minutes each. They were made up of 2-3 other teachers' children, grouped by grades from the 1st through the 7th grade. During this time, teachers whose students were in his PE class had a break.

Well, the day finally came when everything changed for Nancy at Hooper Alexander. It was the day that Mr. Edwards introduced his students to their unit on square dancing. The lesson was a big "to do," especially for a school and district that were just starting to navigate the integration waters. Everyone held their breaths, hoping to avoid any racial skirmishes at a school that was ninety-eight percent white. Mr. Edwards' lesson on square dancing had all the children taking part by using their hands to swing their partner around. Nancy was both alarmed and obstinate as she had no interest in touching anyone nor in having anyone touch her. Mr. Edwards had no idea of what was going on in Nancy's mind or what she was planning.

For the next three days, Nancy was conspicuously absent from school while Mr. Edwards introduced her classmates to square dancing. In her absence, he still assigned Nancy to a group of eight and continued familiarizing her classmates with the dance procedures. The students had fun rehearsing the dance steps. The few black kids in the class added their own personal touches to the standard square-dancing moves. When called out on their modifications, the students said they were adding a little soul!

Finally, Nancy returned to school without a note from her doctor excusing her from participating in PE classes. So, she was not exempt from joining in the activities. After the class completed their warmup exercises, Mr. Edwards called students' names and directed them to their assigned groups. When he called Nancy's name, she said, "I'm not coming!"

This was the first time that Mr. Edwards had really heard Nancy's voice or any student, for that matter, who was defiant.

The class became animated, readying for a playground fight, they began uttering chants of oooooos and ahhhhhhs. Mr. Edwards again called Nancy to join a group, and she said, "No!" even louder.

Mr. Edwards told the class to settle down and to be seated as he attended to Nancy. At that point, Nancy left her seat and ran towards the door to exit the room. Mr. Edwards moved like lightning, intercepting her at the door. Nancy kicked at the door, eventually kicking him before falling to floor with a thud while wailing hysterically. Mr. Edwards was holding the doorknob and quickly bent down to find out why she was crying.

At that moment, Nancy made the decision to trust her teacher, and she began to unravel the towels that she wore daily from around her hands. To Mr. Edwards' surprise, Nancy showed him the secret that she had kept from her classmates. Her hands were different from everyone else's. They were absent of fully developed fingers. As she uncovered her hands, Nancy kept her eyes on Mr. Edwards' eyes. Although he was caught off guard, she noticed that he did not flinch at what she had shown him.

Touched with compassion, Mr. Edwards took Nancy's towels, put them in his pockets, and told her, "Nancy, it's nothing that you or I can do about your fingers. But I can help you to be successful in life. Just trust me." Nancy dried her tears and clung tightly to Mr. Edwards' leg as they walked back over to the rest of the students who were sitting in the large multi-purpose room used as a gym.

As they rejoined the class, Nancy reluctantly got in her assigned group to square dance. When she reached out to her partner to execute one of the steps --- Allemande Left --- the other children could see Nancy hands for the first time. One little boy yelled, "Don't touch me! What's wrong with your hands?" All of the children who saw Nancy's little vestiges of fingers, laughed at her and scattered, not wanting to touch her hands.

Quickly, Mr. Edwards stepped in and calmed the class down, getting them back into their seats. Then, changing from his lesson plan, for the rest of the period, he talked with the students about self-acceptance, accepting Nancy, accepting him, and accepting anyone else who was different from them. When the other teachers came to pick up their students, they could tell that the students were different … unusually quiet. Each teacher asked Mr. Edwards what was wrong with the students. He told them that the children would tell them.

Nancy's homeroom teacher was the last to pick up her students, giving Mr. Edwards more time to talk to her. As she left with her classmates, he took a moment to reflect on what had happened. He took Nancy's towel out of his pockets, and looking at them, he thought about how he could have handled the whole situation better. He also wondered why he wasn't told that Nancy's hands were malformed. He felt that knowing her condition would have prevented him from exposing her secret in such a traumatic way.

Before leaving the school for the day, Mr. Edwards stopped to see the principal to inform him of what had happened between he and Nancy. He was concerned about how Nancy's parents would react when she told them what happened at school. He was alarmed to find out that the principal was unaware of her physical condition as well. At the end of their talk, the principal told Mr. Edwards that he would contact Nancy's parents to bring the events of the day to their attention.

Chapter 24
Anxiety Resolved

Lonnie went home with a lot of anxiety building up, expecting a confrontation with Nancy's parents. He didn't want a fight, but he certainly wouldn't stand for anyone trying to physically beat him up. That night, Lonnie dropped to his knees and prayed for grace and strength as his Grandma Abbie had taught him to do when he didn't know which way to turn.

When Lonnie finally went to bed, he couldn't help but ponder what would happen the next day. Fear crept inside the four walls of his bedroom, making the thumping sound that was pounding in the bottom of his gut. He was thinking that if the school district fired him, he would not only be out of a job, but surely headed to the Vietnam War. He had lottery number #51, a low number in the draft, assuring him that after his birthday came later this year, he would be shipping out to join the military in a month or less. So, Lonnie lay awake for a long time, dreading for the next day to come before he finally drifted off to sleep.

The next day at school, Lonnie was distracted, waiting for the bad news to come at any moment. He kept looking out of the room's windows, and at time, going to his classroom door to look down the hallway, seeing white parents coming in and out the building, trying to guess which ones were Nancy's. All day, he anticipated an explosive encounter with them.

Oddly enough, no one came to see him. While he met some white parents that day, none belonged to Nancy. Three days came and went. He still had a job, and he had not seen Nancy's parents.

So, Mr. Edwards met his gym class as usual. Nancy was present, no longer carrying a towel, and eager to participate in class exercises. As he continued his lesson on self-acceptance and accepting others, Bobby, a spunky, freckled face, red-headed, white boy in the class asked, "Mr. Edwards, are we ever going to do anything else in class besides listen to you preach about being kind to one another?" Mr. Edwards smiled and began to laugh. For him, that was the gut check he needed to resume the square- dancing lesson. So, he assured them that they would do PE exercises the next time that they returned to his class.

As promised, during their next class, Mr. Edwards started where they left off in square dancing. He joined Nancy's group, number #9, and became her partner. When the dance called for the students to "Allemande Left your partner," the children saw Mr. Edwards touch Nancy's hand, and nothing unusual happened. Nancy had fun, and the boys touched her hands with ease as it was now no big deal. That day, Nancy came out of her cocoon and began blossoming as she now no longer had a need for a towel, nor did she feel different from her peers. Other children touched Nancy's hands and treated her like everyone else. She went home that day telling her parents about the fun she had in gym and in square dancing.

Mr. Edwards' square dancing caught on like wildfire. The children could barely contain themselves for wanting to get to gym. Word of the square dancing reached the district office after Mr. Edwards introduced it to the Hooper Alexander teachers in a faculty meeting. They all were doing the "do-si-do" (aka Dosado or DoSaDo.) Mr. Edwards had broken the ice and found acceptance with the staff and the district through square dancing! He now had parents square dancing at a district PTA meeting. No more would white teachers walk pass him looking away at walls. They all stopped to engage him in conversation.

That year, Mr. Edwards grew as a teacher. His on-the-job experiences helped him transition from a rookie to a veteran with his own war stories to tell. The square dance class from Montevallo was paying great dividends in bridging communities. He learned never to surrender to your fears and that a night of prayer could lead to joy in the morning. More importantly, he learned that with children, you must expect the unexpected, as no two days will ever be the same.

Nancy continued to come out of her shell and told Mr. Edwards, "I'm going to be just like other little girls and learn to play the piano." With encouragement and support from her parents, she did! In fact, she played well enough to participate in a piano recital. She also taught herself to type on an old manual typewriter that her parents purchased for her. She mastered typing and had accuracy up to 65 words per minute.

Nancy's social emotional evolution in pictures …..

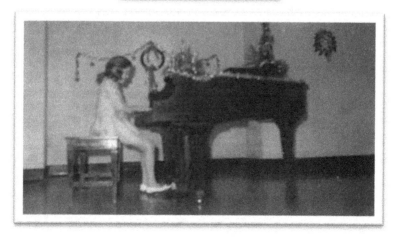

Chapter 25
The Value of Community Engagement

Mr. Edwards' skill as a teacher and acceptance as a leader in the community grew. He not only had the community square dancing, but he also found ways to include the entire community in physical activity. He organized parent-teacher basketball and volleyball games, taking on all parents. Both black and white parents and teachers played together. Mr. Edwards engaged in the sports activities with them, taking open challenges from his students who bragged on their parents' basketball prowess. He whipped them all, and in the process developed a positive reputation in the community and the district. Now, the parents greeted "Mr. Edwards" with a smile.

Lonnie was able to penetrate closed communities, establish positive relationships, bridge differences, and enhance personal relations, using his basketball talents to open doors that were traditionally closed, allowing him to bond with professional athletes.

Lonnie signed his first contract as a professional basketball player with Quixie Quackers, a local semi-professional team in Georgia promoted by radio station WQXI. His jump shot never left him without making its mark upon those who would rise to the challenge. His skills and noteworthy accomplishments earned him four Basketball Hall of Fame inductions in Mississippi and Alabama. Lonnie's basketball ability transcended the collegiate Halls of Fame as he found himself in his later years on a team that dominated in their age category in the Senior Olympics for which qualification starts at 50 years of age. They won the Gold Medal!

As Lonnie's athletic fame in the school district and the community took off, so did his professional career. He returned to the University of Montevallo, joined by Hansell, as both earned double master's degrees in Physical Education and School Administration.

Back in DeKalb, Lonnie's interpersonal skills led to his being utilized as a transformational leader. After four years as a teacher, he was promoted to the position of Assistant Principal (AP) and was assigned to several elementary schools to help address racial tensions and racial relations there. Lonnie's first assignment as AP was at Gresham Park. His second assignment had him returning to Hooper Alexander, and his third was Leslie Steele. His stint at each lasted a year, and at each, he was successful in building and improving the school's culture as well as race relations in the schools and their communities.

His positive influence at the schools and in the community caught the eye of the Superintendent and other senior administrators. As a result, he was promoted to Personnel Counselor, making him the first black person to work in the DeKalb County School District's Human Resources Department. Since the school system was under a court-ordered segregation decree, and with the demographics of its staff and students making the district almost 99% white, a lot of work would be required to comply with the guidelines. Lonnie felt that being placed in this position in Human Resources was as if he was given the keys to the DeKalb leadership Maserati. Now, he had to keep it on the road, take it in a new direction, and make everyone proud of his driving without crashing or causing major accidents. But he was prepared for this moment and was ready to help steer the district on a different path!

Lonnie knew that creating a winning culture in DeKalb started with building the culture up and not tearing it down! He also knew that a key component of building it up was adding to it "winning" employees who had successful track records with students in the classroom as well as with parents and other leaders in communities in which they served. One of these new *winning* employees turned out to be Hansell Gunn, Jr.

Chapter 26
The Graduates Return Home to Montevallo

In Alabama, everyone was taking notice of a rookie junior high school coach, Hansell Gunn, Jr., who had taken two failing athletic programs, which had no previous histories of winning, and had made them champions. Hansell was revered by his schools and their communities as he had clearly separated himself from his peers by creating a winning culture. Pizitz Middle School wanted to keep him as the stakeholders were begging for more. But they couldn't hold on as the rookie coach who, looking like a free agent, headed for the open market.

While at Piztiz, Hansell continued to prepare himself for that next big thing. During those two years, both he and Lonnie kept their promise to the University of Montevallo's Dean of Education by keeping their noses to the grind and by returning to Montevallo for graduate school. While on campus, Hansell and Lonnie saw, first-hand, the fruits of their sacrifice as more black students now permeated the campus. On the occasions in which they had opportunities to talk with these students, they were embraced and thanked for the sacrifices they made in coming to Montevallo.

Staff mixer at Pizitz Middle School

Unlike when they first arrived, when they were the only two black male student-athletes, now a sizable number of male and female students of color populated the campus. This time, Hansell noticed that in addition to more students of color, there were more black people on campus working in various office positions. Lonnie and Hansell were very pleased and encouraged to see how progressive the campus had become.

Their evolution in the integration process hit full bloom upon returning to the Montevallo campus for graduate school. When Lonnie and Hansell returned to their alma mater, they rented a home for the summer. Drs. Frank and Bobbye Lightfoot were professors at the college who embraced them as their own sons. Although they were a white family, they were more than a mom and dad away from home. They, along with Dr. Leon Davis, were always available for advice and counsel through the years – as undergraduate and graduate students. Lonnie and Hansell were also heavily supported by the black community of Montevallo. They were fed by some of the best "chefs" and served as role models to the young children in the neighborhoods. They had truly come full circle as their outlook on life, race relations, and human relations would be forever shaped by their Montevallo bonds.

Chapter 27
The Glenn High Hawks' Transformation

When Hansell finished graduate school, he felt that he still had some unfinished business with basketball. In his mind, he had one more river to cross before he would let go – becoming a Head Basketball Coach at a high school. He had set his sights on a bigger stage, and he knew that he had to strike while the iron was hot. He saw an opportunity to grow during the summer before his third year at Pitziz. It was at Glenn High School, a nearby predominantly black school in the city of Birmingham. Hansell believed that obtaining a head coaching job was within his reach. He believed that the time had come!

Nevertheless, being selected at the Head Coach at a high school was not an easy task as Hansell's critics were not ready to grant this request, knocking his age, not his race. The consensus among his coaching peers was that Hansell was too young and lacked the experience necessary for such a responsibility; after all, he was only twenty-three years old. But Hansell was not dissuaded by his naysayers. His time at Montevallo and his early success at Piztiz bolstered his confidence. He was determined to not let anything, or anyone, easily keep him from achieving his goal.

Hansell went on several interviews for head coaching jobs. The rejections came fast and furious. Sometimes he barely had a chance to sit down before he heard the "No" response. The knock from the interviewing principal was that he lacked seasoning. His winning at the junior high school was not enough to get him serious consideration. After all, Hansell would just be a few years older than his students. Hansell had not considered age as a factor in their rejecting him but was determined to pursue any rising vacancy.

Glenn High School had already turned Hansell down, but their vacancy had still not been filled. His Montevallo experience taught him that persistence paid great dividends. So, while keeping this goal in mind, Hansell continued to "bloom where he was planted." Very soon he found favor with a white senior administrator in his school district whose grandson played on his championship teams and who spoke highly of Coach Gunn.

That vote of confidence earned Hansell an audience with that district leader. After their meeting, the district leader was not only impressed with Coach Gunn's positive impact upon his grandson but also with his temperament, his skills, and his ability to hold his own in the almost all-white setting. As a result, Hansell was appointed as the new Head Boys' Basketball Coach at Glenn High School.

Hansell was confident that he would do an excellent job. But first, he had to meet his students since he accepted both a high school teaching job and the Head Coaching position. He arrived at Glenn High early on the first day of school to get acclimated to his new setting. He had not had an opportunity to meet his players nor even build a roster. For Hansell, it was like being back at Fifth Street High but with two major differences this time --- the school was bigger, and all eyes would be on him.

Hansell welcomed the opportunity to be back in the gym again. He took in the moment by grabbing a basketball and engaging in a routine shoot around like his college days. Hansell was always comfortable on the perimeter, and the former Fifth Street Bomber took any opportunity to launch those thirty-foot shots to the sweet sound of "swish" with music from his transistor radio playing in the background. As his students began to file in the gym, while heading to the locker room, they could not help but notice the music playing and this tall stringy black man about their age with the big popcorn afro hitting jump shots from all over the court. They had no idea that Hansell was their new Physical Education teacher.

The first day was upbeat as Hansell was a clear hit based on reactions from students in the hallways, at the water fountains, in the restrooms, and in the cafeteria. He had made a positive impression. All day long, Hansell captivated his students' interest from the time they walked inside the gym. They all noticed the same thing, music playing and Hansell hitting long-range jump shots.

Young, personable, Hansell captured the student's attention when he spoke to them in his calm tone. After he posted the notice for basketball tryouts, the Glenn High boys responded. Gunn had several veterans returning from the previous winning season. He looked forward to helping them continue their winning ways and working with the new hungry boys seeking their taste of championship gold.

Coach Gunn and his team hit the ground running . He wanted to make Glenn a powerhouse, and he knew that would take some work. His players were trainable and eager to get to work. Gunn knew all eyes would be on him to keep the team in winning form.

		1974 Regional Tournament	
	Glenn	116-65	Mortimer Jordan
mi	Glenn	89-44	Leeds
ials	Glenn	82-44	Hewitt-Trussville
ials	Glenn	94-83	Fairfield
		1974 State Tournament	
1	Glenn	90-66	Tuskegee Insti
Semi	Glenn	105-87	Guntersville
Finals	Glenn	98-69	Russellville

That summer, Coach Gunn's boys went to camp and learned to play ball the Coahoma and Montevallo way. Hansell added some nuances to the playbook that the other coaches did not have. He taught his players to use sign language to direct the offense and defense. Hansell had transposed the signs he learned playing baseball at Montevallo and incorporated them into his basketball program. It proved successful at Vestavia Junior High, leading to back-to-back middle school basketball championships and a baseball championship in his first two years.

Hansell's players quickly caught on to the signing. For the onlookers, it appeared that the team was running on automatic pilot as no one ever saw Coach Gunn yelling at his players. He and his point guard exchanged signs throughout the game, and in turn, the guard relayed the plays to the team.

They became a combination, lean and mean, showtime, defensive unit with a high- octane offense, not like anything their region or conference had ever seen before. Coach Gunn unleashed his team and watched them smother and devour the competition... game after game. The team, nicknamed the Green Machine, capped off a perfect 36-0 season and won the State Championship title in the Alabama State Basketball Tournament. With this win, Coach Gunn obtained instant legendary status.

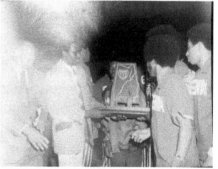

Having the state championship under his belt, the accolades for this shy, Division 3A coach continued. His team's undefeated winning streak kept him in the public eye as his team's activities were almost a daily read in the local newspaper. Coach Gunn was recognized everywhere he went and became a local celebrity. He was named Coach of the Year, climaxing an awesome third year of coaching and a first year as a high school coach. Coach Gunn's teams continued to achieve an elevated level of performance at Glenn with consistent post-season play and multiple final four appearances.

After eight years of coaching, the Glenn High Hawk spread his wings and took flight for new nesting grounds yet knowing one day he would always return home.

Chapter 28
Soaring To New A Nesting Ground

After earning dual master's degrees in Educational Leadership and Supervision and Physical Education, both Lonnie and Hansell set their sights on their new career paths. Hansell continued to hone his teaching craft in the classroom before reaching out to his friend, Lonnie, who had already broken through the school leadership ranks as an Assistant Principal and had recently been promoted to the position of Personnel Administrator. Hansell saw his best opportunity for a leadership position coming in a much larger school system. So, he contacted Lonnie and completed an application with the DeKalb County School District.

DeKalb administrators who interviewed Hansell were impressed with this Montevallo alum. One of his interviews was with the principal at Peachtree High School. He was looking for a new Assistant Principal (AP) who could mesh with the Peachtree Community. Students of color had just started attending Peachtree, so it was a school in transition. Hansell's calm demeanor and soft tone were just what his new school needed because as AP, he would coordinate school-wide attendance and discipline.

The interview went well as Hansell walked the campus and shared stories of Montevallo and Vestavia with the principal who knew right away that Hansell would be a perfect fit for his operation. So, he made the recommendation to the Human Resources department, and Hansell was hired.

Hansell performed and developed well as an Assistant Principal. His public speaking class at Montevallo and his successful coaching experience at Piztiz Middle and Glenn High School paid off. His coaching not only prepared him to succeed in the sports arena, but it also prepared him for handling diversity and serving in leadership roles.
Hansell was no stranger to easing a community through the

integration process. As a result, he quickly bonded with his new Peachtree family. During the next four years, he built smooth, seamless human relation bridges, connecting all students and stakeholders associated with Peachtree High School.

Chapter 29
Changing the Landscape from Within

In rebuilding the district's culture, Lonnie, once again, turned to athletics to bring the players together. He began the process by uniting the group that was critical to the district's overall operational effectiveness, the school administrators. This group, for the most part, was miles apart in geographical areas, but more importantly in working together. They operated more like strangers. Lonnie knew that they had to come together for effective team building and collaboration to take place. So, with the support of then school superintendent Dr. Robert Freeman, Lonnie organized a district-wide basketball game with administrators.

This would be the first time the district would see the superintendent in casual attire. Dr. Freeman worked the sidelines serving as coach. Hansell's assignment at Peachtree enabled him to reunite and play basketball with Lonnie in the district organized administrator's game. Both Lonnie and Hansell were on Dr. Freeman's team.

The game was held on the campus of DeKalb Community College, a midway point uniting both the north and south ends of the DeKalb school system, in front of a packed crowd. Both Lonnie and Hansell brought a lot of energy and fun to the contest. In the end, the superintendent's team won with Lonnie leading all scorers. More importantly, the lines of communication were opened, and the walls of isolation and indifference came down that separated many members of DeKalb's leadership team. Afterwards, the district's administrators began having rich, meaningful conversations which led to joint initiatives and more collaboration when implementing academic programs that connected a once divided student body, curriculum, and population.

Lonnie continued to develop plans to help the district grow. That involved his participation in retooling the district and his continuing to grow professionally as well. Over the next seventeen years in DeKalb County School District's Human Resources Department, Lonnie crisscrossed the southeastern United States, looking high and low for teachers at job fairs and on college campuses. His recruitment locations included many Historically Black Colleges and Universities (HBCUs) to find great candidates for the system and to help contribute to the diversity it was now seeking. Additionally, based on the results of his doctoral dissertation, Lonnie influenced the district to focus on developing teachers within. He led the establishment of future teacher recruitment programs at the district's high schools to inspire and to encourage the youth to choose the teaching profession as a career.

While toiling in the field of Education, enduring a sunup to sundown schedule like he experienced on his family's farm, while also marrying and having a family, Lonnie made the time to pursue a doctorate degree, preparing himself for future executive leadership positions. However, adhering to the sage advice to "Bloom where you're planted," he actively worked to change and update district policies, procedures, and norms to facilitate fairness and more career opportunities for all employees, especially people of color.

Lonnie receiving his doctorate degree from Atlanta University, 1987

Through it all, he became an alumnus of the Atlanta University (AU) doctoral program, earning the title of **Dr.** Lonnie Edwards. AU is now CAU – Clark Atlanta University.

As the years rolled by, Lonnie's career advanced. His education, training, and experiences equipped him to serve in many positions in the district. Over the course of time, Lonnie wore numerous hats, moving from a classroom teacher to an Assistant Principal, then transitioning to "central administration," where he served as a Personnel Counselor, Personnel Administrator, and Assistant Director of Personnel in Human Resources. After seventeen years in this department, he was promoted to an Assistant Superintendent, a position which could be compared to a leading point guard and floor general, controlling the flow of the game. Under this title, his assignments varied.

They included coordinating Instruction and Curriculum; Community and Staff Relations; Parent, Community, and Support Programs; Business Affairs; and Elementary Administration. He also served as a Clark Atlanta Adjunct Professor and part-time real estate agent for many years. For Lonnie, his life was as if he were back on the farm again, with plenty of chores to do and with little time for sleep. But this time, he had a support team to help get the jobs done!

Alice Ann Hamilton, Director Personnel

(L-R) Lonnie Edwards, Barbara Cooper, and Bobby Stephens

Chapter 30
When a Child Speaks

Recognition and adulation would follow Lonnie as it clearly appeared that his star was rising. Dr. Lonnie J. Edwards, Sr. had become a highly respected educator, motivational speaker, and published author.

Dr. and Mrs. Lonnie (Cynthia) Edwards in New York, NY

Unexpectedly, one of Lonnie's former students, wrote the nationally syndicated television program, the Sally Jessy Raphael Show, filmed in New York City, in response to the show's solicitation of people who wanted to thank someone on national television for changing their lives. His young student who resisted taking part in square dancing, some 25 years before, wrote about him, calling him the teacher that changed her life.

Then, married with five children, Nancy Johnson Miller, no longer covered her hands to hide the vestiges of fingers with which she was born. She had become a very outgoing, self-assured woman who had and used an abundance of skills.

About a year after she sent her letter to the Sally Jessy Raphael Show, she was contacted by one of their staff members to ascertain whether this would be a story that they would air. After Nancy recounted the story of her, as a 10-year-old child, inadvertently being confronted with revealing her secret --- malformed hands ---by a new black male

Dr. Edwards and former student, Nancy Miller, being reunited on the Sally Jessy Raphael Show

teacher at her school, the show decided to include her story as one of the segments on "Thank You For Changing My Life."

Nancy said that she had lost touch with Mr. Edwards, so she was asked to come on to the show to make an appeal to the audience to help her find him. Little did Nancy know that the show's staff found Lonnie in the DeKalb County School District, talked with him to confirm her account of their story, and afterwards, arranged to reunite them on national television. His appearance was to be a surprise to Nancy. Their reconnection was a powerful testimony on the value of the classroom teacher! Happy hugs were exchanged, and tears were flowing, not only from them but also from many audience members! Their reunion may be viewed on YouTube using the following link:
https://youtu.be/PefCiwZjF34

Lonnie and Nancy's visit in New York City ultimately changed both of their lives. It inspired Lonnie to become a champion for children with special needs.

A Teacher's Touch: Reaching Beyond Boundaries

Lonnie J. Edwards Sr., Ed. D.

He also penned a book, **'A Teacher's Touch: Reaching Beyond Boundaries,** telling the story of this chance encounter, as a young, first year, Physical Education teacher, with a student who had hidden the abnormality of her hands from other teachers and fellow students for years and how she overcame this social emotional challenge.

In my interview with Lonnie for this book, he reflected on his appearance on the Sally Jessy Raphael Show with Nancy. He told me that he was indeed touched by Nancy's outreach to say, "Thanks," for what he considered to just be doing the right thing --- showing concern, empathy, and compassion for a child deeply affected by a physical disorder that she hid from others. Lonnie shared that he was extremely disappointed that no one, neither a parent nor a staff member, had made him aware of Nancy's malformed hands. On the other hand, he said that he seriously doubted that anyone else knew of her condition at the school. Nancy had become adept at concealing and using a variety of tactics to cover and hide her hands. Academically, she was a good student. So, without extra personal attention directed from teachers to her, her maneuvers made it possible for her to get by and for her hands to go unnoticed.

But backstage, after the Sally Show, Lonnie took the opportunity to ask Nancy questions that had stayed in the back of his mind whenever he thought of the traumatic unveiling of her hands during the square dance routine years ago. He asked her, "Where are your parents? Why didn't they come to the school after the incident that exposed your hands?"

Nancy stated that her father was deceased and that her mother lived in Cottondale, Florida. When Lonnie asked Nancy if she would get her mother on the telephone, she did. It was his first time ever speaking with her mother, Ms. Betty Johnson. During their brief conversation, Lonnie agreed to visit her. It would be the first time that they would have met in more than twenty-five (25) years.

A few weeks later, Lonnie and his wife, Cynthia, along with a public relations representative and videographer headed to Cottondale, FL for the visit with Ms. Johnson and to record it. Lonnie was uncertain of how the visit would go, but he was looking forward to it. He had so many questions about the family's reaction once they found that Nancy's secret had been exposed at school.

When they arrived, Ms. Johnson greeted Lonnie and the other guests warmly. She was incredibly happy to see Lonnie and embraced him with open arms, although she was in an advanced stage of emphysema and connected to an oxygen tank.

Ms. Johnson's words of thanks were filled with humility as she told the visitors that she had always prayed for Lonnie. She went on to say that he had risked his life to help her child. Sitting at the kitchen table, with a bowed head and a deep sigh, she looked at Lonnie and said, "Thank God for you. We left Nancy alone to make it the best that she could. She had no allies at school until you came along." As she continued to chat, she shared that she noticed that her husband's handkerchiefs kept disappearing and that she didn't know why until Nancy told her about the incident. Then, she found that she was using them to wrap around her hands. However, after her hands were revealed, although not by choice, Nancy no longer covered them, and handkerchiefs stopped disappearing!

Acknowledging that her health condition had worsened, Ms. Johnson said that she had asked God to let her live long enough to say thanks to Lonnie. Lonnie, Cynthia, and their friends spent the day with Ms. Johnson, her sister, Nancy, and her son. It was an enjoyable time and a revealing, emotional, and heartwarming experience.

Ms. Betty Johnson reflecting on Lonnie's support of her daughter, Nancy

 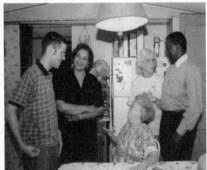

Photos from Lonnie and Cynthia's visit with Ms. Betty Johnson, her sister, and her grandson.

About six months later, Ms. Johnson passed. Nancy called Lonnie and Cynthia to inform them of her loss and to ask them to join her and their family at her mother's homegoing services. She also asked Lonnie to be one of the pallbearers at the funeral. So, Lonnie, Cynthia, and another couple traveled to Florida to pay honor to Ms. Johnson and to support Nancy during this chapter in her life. While there, they were introduced to Nancy's two brothers and other students from their days at Hooper-Alexander Elementary School. Lonnie remembered them as children but did not know that they were related to Nancy until then!

During the writing of this book, Nancy was living in Leesburg, FL and she, Lonnie, and Cynthia were in frequent contact with each other. However, Nancy passed on April 1, 2022, prior to the book being published.

Lonnie feels that his experience with Nancy is a good representation of the impact that most teachers have on their students. It also highlights the value of the classroom teacher. Although few students stop to say, "Thank you," most live in a state of eternal gratitude.

The following year after the appearance on the Sally Jessy Raphael Show, in 1997, Lonnie and Cynthia, along with a good friend, Dr. Thomas Smith, formed a not-for-profit foundation to award college scholarships to students with physical challenges. They named it the Edwards-Miller Foundation for Physical Disabilities, honoring Nancy's elevating their teacher-student interaction to a national level.

Each year at the foundation's annual fundraiser, Nancy would attend. She and Lonnie would share their story, along with the video from the Sally Show, prior to presenting scholarships to deserving students. In its eleven (11) years of operation, the Edwards- Miller Foundation awarded scholarships to twenty (20) students who attended colleges all over the USA.

Lonnie and Nancy receiving a copy of the Atlanta Journal Constitution's article about their teacher-student interaction at a reception hosted by executives with the Hyatt Regency Buckhead, Atlanta, GA

THURSDAY, OCT. 10, 1996

The Atlanta Journal-Constitution

Local News

LOCAL NEWS

A teacher's inspiring legacy

JEAN SHIFRIN / Staff

Nancy Johnson Miller returned Wednesday to Hooper Alexander Elementary School, where, as a fifth-grader 25 years ago, she met physical education teacher Lonnie Edwards. By encouraging her not to be ashamed of having most of her fingers missing, Edwards helped her be all she could be, she told a small group that had arranged the emotional homecoming. Edwards, now an assistant superintendent for the DeKalb County school system, noted that most of those at the reunion were crying, but "I used up my tears," in the last two weeks, since the TV show "Sally Jessy Raphael" brought the two back together. But by the time he finished speaking, he too was in tears. Hugging Miller, he advised the gathering, "Be careful what you say to fifth-graders."

Chapter 31
Searching for His Purpose

While Lonnie's career was advancing, Hansell began hungering for more challenging opportunities, too. He also had bloomed where he was planted, but his desire to lead was pressing him.

Hansell was bitten by the leadership bug and being Assistant Principal did not satisfy the fire that burned inside. So, he thanked Lonnie for paving the way for his coming to DeKalb, but also told him that it was time for him to seek other opportunities.

SHRINE ON DISPLAY — Thomasville Exchange Club helps Douglass Middle School celebrate the 200th birthday of the United States Constitution by dedicating a Freedom Shrine at the school Tuesday. Present for the dedication are (L-R) past president of the Georgia District Exchange Clubs Alex Crittenden, Douglass Principal Hansell Gunn, club president Robert Milberg and club member Jim Hay. The shrine is a display of 28 historic American documents, including the Constitution and the Bill of Rights, which Exchange Clubs of America have installed by the thousands in public buildings across the country.

Presentation to Principal Hansell Gunn Jr. from Thomasville Exchange Club Members

After four years of serving in the DeKalb County School District, Hansell left for an opportunity as a principal in the Fulton County School System. The governor of the state of Georgia at the time knew the school administrators in Thomasville, GA, and highly recommended him for the position of Principal at Douglas Middle School in Thomasville, Georgia.

Douglas was a small, low achieving middle school with only grades seven and eight and whose student population and staff were both largely African American. Hansell happily accepted the offer and spent his time there mending broken fences not only between the students but also between black and white people in the community.

The Coach, Hansell Gunn, Scores On Former Player And New NBA Superstar, Andrew Toney

At Douglas, Hansell continued to grow as a leader and, with his team, transformed the school. Test scores increased, and the school climate changed for the better. However, after five years, Hansell sought, found, and left for a more challenging opportunity.

Hansell's leadership journey kept him on the move in Georgia as he was not ready to return to Mississippi just yet. Looking for a new opportunity in which he could make a difference, Hansell reconnected with Lonnie who was now at the senior executive level in the DeKalb County School District (DCSD). After discussing his personal and professional goals as well as the current employment opportunities in DeKalb with Lonnie, Hansell decided to return to DCSD and applied for positions there. He interviewed and was selected to serve as an Assistant Principal at Peachtree Charter Middle School. During his time at Peachtree, Hansell completed his Specialist degree from Jacksonville State University, Jacksonville, Alabama as well as all of his coursework toward his doctorate, earning the status of "all but dissertation," (ABD). Hansell felt the doctoral accomplishments would position him for greater opportunities later down the road.

In 1989, Hansell was selected to serve as Principal of Benjamin E. Banneker High School. This school, located in southwest Atlanta, had a student population which was more than 90 percent African American. Banneker was considered a "failing school" with low teacher morale and daily student fights. Nevertheless, Hansell was excited about another opportunity to make his mark; so, he approached the job at Banneker with a clear vision. He knew what he wanted his school to look and feel like. Therefore, he marshalled his staff and secured resources to fill in the blanks as he painted a new picture for the school.

Tanya, Lisa, Jacob, and Keesha

Principal Gunn and pupil

Mrs. Morrow and Michelle

Christy and Charlene

First, Hansell built a consensus with the learning community – students, faculty, and staff. Second, he did a SWOT analysis to identify the school's strengths, weaknesses, opportunities, and threats. Third, he and his leadership team, with buy-in from all staff and teachers, developed plans to address the findings in the needs assessment. This soft-spoken man was now charging full speed ahead as a change agent with his initiatives.

Principal Gunn with Banneker High School Staff

In just one-year, Hansell implemented his plan to improve teacher morale, decrease fights, and put discipline issues on the decline. With the support of this school's learning community, Hansell hit paydirt! The school saw a steady rise in the student enrollment as it was one of 24 public schools named to the Georgia Schools of Excellence Program. This award recognizes high-achieving schools as well as those making the greatest gains.

One school in each category is recognized in each Congressional district in Georgia, based on five pillars: content mastery, school climate, operations, environmental and sustainability education, and innovation.

Banneker High School in College Park, under the leadership of Principal Hansell Gunn.

During his five years at Banneker, Hansell etched out a legacy as a change agent. He would not soon be forgotten as he watched his students from a failing school environment beginning to soar academically, developing school pride, and going off to college. Banneker also was awarded the Blue-Ribbon Award of Excellence, having gone from worst to first. With this award, the U.S. Department of Education honors elementary, middle, and high schools that are either academically superior or demonstrate significant gains in student achievement. Schools nominated by the Georgia Department of Education attend a ceremony in Washington, D.C.

Principal Gunn with Banneker High School Staff

This recognition helped to restore school and community pride while opening doors for the school in the form of partnerships with the business community and highly visible associations with the professional sports teams in the city.

However, at the end of the school year Hansell and his wife, Wilda, went out west.

he Atlanta Journal / The Atlanta Constitution **METRO & STATE**

Banneker ranked in top 24 schools

From troubled to state's elite in single year

By Angela Duerson Tuck
STAFF WRITER

What does it take to become a Georgia School of Excellence? In Banneker High School's case, it took a complete makeover.

When Hansell Gunn was hired last year as principal of the College Park school, teacher morale was at rock bottom, fights were routine and unhappy parents were pulling their children out in favor of voluntary busing elsewhere.

Mr. Gunn called for drastic changes. He instituted an extended-day program for students who needed help meeting graduation requirements, started an awards program to boost student morale and began a mentoring program for male pupils from single-parent families.

In one year, Banneker has gone from having the worst discipline record in Fulton County to having one of the best. As a result, Mr. Gunn said, parents brought their children back, boosting enrollment from 864 last year to 1,150.

"Once we changed the school climate, everything else fell into place," says Hansell Gunn, who was hired one year ago.

DWIGHT ROSS JR. / Staff

"We've come together as a family for one cause," said Mr. Gunn. "Once we changed the school climate, everything else fell into place."

On Tuesday, Banneker got another boost when it became one of 24 public schools named Georgia Schools of Excellence.

The annual competition evaluates schools based on leadership, innovative education programs and student outcomes.

A panel of Tennessee educators considered 67 applicants for honors that could go to one elementary, one middle/junior high and one high school from each of the state's ten congressional districts, and chose to select 24 for the 30 possible honors.

Wilda was offered a great career opportunity in Denver, Colorado. So, after accepting the offer, she and Hansell made the move to a new locale. Over the next seven years, Hansell served as Assistant Principal at Wheatridge Middle, then West Middle School. At Montbello High School, he served as Principal. All of these schools provided the leadership rigor that he wanted.

The Montbello Warrior Times March 15, 2022

Mr. Gunn, the Super Star Principal
By Amber Brown

Mr. Gunn made his debut with the community when he was interviewed with CDM, (Collaborative Decision Making committee) last summer. According to a CDM representative, Hansel Gunn was the best candidate for principal at Montbello. "He has the right ideas and I'm excited to have him running my son's school," said Mary Sam.

This year's new principal is from Atlanta Georgia. He is the father of two children. His daughter, Leslie, recently graduated from college. Mr. Gunn's son, Jonathan, is a senior in high school.

Mr. Gunn and counselor Danielle Dillard

Tangenika Davenport voted most spirited senior poses with Amanda Ferguson

Mr. Gunn has been a principal for twenty-two years and has thirty years in the educational field. Over the past years, Mr. Gunn has worked in four different schools as head principal.

According to Mrs. Duffy, who is Mr. Gunn's assistant, Gunn has made substantial improvements at West Middle School and a high school in Atlanta, Ga.

Students inspired him to come to Montbello. Mr. Gunn said he wants to help students make a positive change in their lives. The new principal is committed to changing the negative image of Montbello.

Many teachers and staff are impressed with Mr. Gunn's ability to run the school smoothly. However, he does not take full credit for a great year so far.

When Mr. Gunn came to Montbello he expected to find a great staff, caring community, and a committed student body.

Ms. Dickson and Ms. Lorbeer enjoying the day at a game

Improving and Impacting the Academic Achievement of Minority Students by Empowering Teachers

Hansell Gunn

This young boy, now a man, was light years away from his origins in Egypt, Mississippi, and he was doing what he always wanted to do --- making a difference. Hansell immersed himself in the new culture and the diversity in Colorado. He found himself busy, but as always, on the lookout for new opportunities. They often seemed just around the corner, and he didn't want to miss them!

Chapter 32
Addressing the Racial Divide and Ensuring Inclusion

Back in Georgia, Dr. Lonnie Edwards had become a well-known and well-respected leader in the DeKalb County School District as well as in the metro-Atlanta community. It was Lonnie's grass roots, hands-on approach to leadership that kept him focused on meeting the needs of the district. Using collaborative skills, he worked with the district's leadership team to develop and implement practices and policies that enabled the school system to balance the racial divide through attrition and purposeful hiring practices. When Lonnie arrived in the district's Human Resources Department, he was the only person of color there amidst forty-three white people. However, by the time he left, through effective communication and collaboration, he had contributed to creating and instituting guidelines and policies which equalized the working environment. Lonnie would say that "success is found in the repetition of our failures" as he was never afraid of failing. He was always willing to take the shot, hit or miss.

As Lonnie worked to balance the staff in the Human Resources Department, he also addressed the issues of desegregation and teacher shortage in the district. He developed and implemented a para-professional program that stocked the district with a diverse, steady, and ready in-house supply of teacher support personnel. They were employed and completing teacher requirement classes that allowed them to transition into classroom teachers, thus helping to close the racial divide.

Once a change agent, always a change agent. Another change credited to Lonnie was incorporating the United Negro College Fund (UNCF) into the DeKalb County School District Foundation's list of charitable organizations. For several years, Lonnie helped to organize a day of volleyball and basketball games at local high schools as fundraisers for the UNCF. He played in the basketball games. Each year, this day of play raised between $2,000 - $3000 in funds for UNCF. However, Lonnie felt that, as a District, they could do more. Looking for new ways to expand the UNCF fundraising activities, he discovered the district's charitable organization that was supported through payroll deduction. Through it, employees could select a non-profit to support and contribute to it on a bi-weekly or monthly basis.

Learning about this avenue for contributing, Lonnie contacted the district's charitable organization to discuss adding the UNCF. Talking with its staff, he found out that the UNCF had been considered in the past, but the foundation's board had never given approval to add it to the official list for accepting contributions. Researching more about this process, Lonnie was informed that the UNCF had been denied being put on the list for three consecutive years. It was also brought to his attention that the foundation board had only one black person on it. After learning these facts, Lonnie decided to attend an upcoming foundation board meeting. His rank in the district earned him a cordial welcome.

After being recognized as a guest, he went right to the point. He asked the board why the UNCF was not being considered as an organization to which employees could donate. The chair of the board said that it was a bonding issue --- the UNCF needed to be bonded. A bonded treasurer adds assurance to an investor or donor that his/her money is safe with a company or an organization.

Since Lonnie did not know about the UNCF's bonding plan, he requested a 24-hour delay to provide him an opportunity to explore that concern. His request was granted and within 3 hours, Lonnie had secured the confirmation from the local UNCF Regional Office that it was indeed bonded for $200,000. He went to the UNCF office to personally pick up the bonding document and presented it to the foundation board the next day. It was accepted, and the United Negro College Fund became #81 on the district's charitable list.

What a monumental, "silent" breakthrough for Historically Black Colleges and Universities (HBCUs).

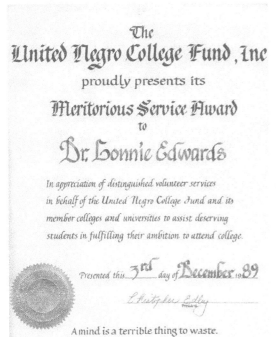

Lonnie and the DeKalb County Board of Education were recognized and honored by the UNCF for their support. Since payroll deduction was authorized at the district for UNCF, hundreds of thousands of dollars have been contributed to the organization by the DeKalb County School District's employees. A Huge Victory!

When the final buzzer sounded ending Lonnie's career in DeKalb after 34 years, the man from Shaw, Mississippi had left it all on the floor, leaving behind a legacy not easily to be forgotten. But, for Lonnie, the work and contributions to society didn't end there!

EVENTS & ACTIVITIES

A Legacy of Leadership and Service

Guests attending Dr. Edwards' retirement party.

The King of Kindness Retires

After 33 years of excellent service to the DeKalb County School System, Dr. Lonnie Edwards recently retired. Edwards, who lives in Stone Mountain, began teaching in 1971. He rose to be assistant superintendent in the school system.

In 1996, he attained national prominence when a former student, Nancy Miller, sought the help of the "Sally Jesy Raphael Show" to locate the teacher who had inspired her to participate in life, despite being born with a deformed hand. Miller wanted to thank Edwards for helping change her

life 25 years before. She recounted the story of how he encouraged her to rise above her handicap and participate in school and life.

Today, she is a successful professional. Dr. Edwards is continuing to help students with special needs with the Edwards Miller Foundation, which grants scholarships to youths with disabilities.

After retiring in 2004 from the DeKalb County School District, Dr. Lonnie J. Edwards, Sr. was celebrated for a job well done, but he still had a ball in his hand. Contrary to those who retire looking for the rocking chair to rock the time away, Lonnie was called out of retirement with no time to get used to a rocking chair and a glass of lemonade! He was contacted by a New York school district to aid them in managing a crisis. They wanted their employees to value and manage diversity more effectively. So, after meeting with Lonnie, they engaged him as a consultant. He met with his educational consulting team of all-star professionals, Edwards & Associates, Inc., and they headed to the Big Apple! Game on!

Edwards & Associates, Inc. was given an opportunity to help resolve an issue affecting race relations and racial perceptions which had caused an uproar not only among the school system's staff, but also in the community that it served. This was clearly an area in which Lonnie and his team could help. They were a diverse group of educators with expertise and experiences in conducting action research; curriculum design and analysis; race relations; data compilation; system analysis; interviewing and fact-finding; human relations; managing diversity, equity, and inclusion; school leadership ... and more.

At the end of the engagement in New York, Edwards & Associates had helped to mend the professional and personal relationships that had been shattered, and the school system had begun to put systems in place to address the weaknesses and threats identified in the consultants' analysis. The school system's leadership stepped up to the responsibility to proactively mitigate any future race-related problems.

Fresh from a successful engagement in the Big Apple, Lonnie felt a call to action once more. This time, he sought a position with the Georgia State Department of Education (GDOE) and was offered a challenging assignment with Title I Programs as a Federal Programs Education Specialist for all private schools in Georgia. This was a newly created position. Again, Lonnie found himself as a lone black man in a sea of white faces as he crisscrossed the state, merging into a new culture as he carried the Title I message.

The Title I, Part A Program is the largest federal program supporting both elementary and secondary education. The program's resources are allocated based upon the poverty rates of students enrolled in schools and districts and are designed to help ensure that all children meet challenging state academic standards. The funding supplies supplemental instruction for students who are economically disadvantaged or are at risk of failing to meet state standards.

Taking the Title I message throughout the state forced Lonnie to dig deep within his skills toolbox to bridge cultural differences, gain acceptance, and have his message of compliance heard. After three years, Lonnie left the Georgia Department of Education in good hands with an impeccable record, and his department was recognized as having ensured that the state, for the first time, successfully followed the federal guidelines for the Title I program for private schools. After a federal audit, no violations were found and no recommendations for improvement were made! Another win!

Chapter 33
Going Back to His Roots to Take the Mantle

Hansell heeded the call to return home to West Point, Mississippi to be near his aging mother, Clytee. He had now come full circle as a student and school leader as he accepted the principalship at his former school, Fifth Street Junior High. This was a humbling experience for Hansell as he was now given an opportunity to make a difference in his own community. So, he rolled up his sleeves and reported to work. In his first official act, he removed an old rusted barbed wire fence which surrounded the school and replaced it with a wrought iron one. With just one stroke, he implemented a successful campus beautification initiative, never to be forgotten.

Hansell's tenure at Fifth Street lasted only a year as the Okolona Board of Education offered him a more hands-on and fulfilling role in the district. He received a 3-2 nod to become the Superintendent of Schools for the Okolona School District, in his own backyard. The district had grown some since the days of his youth. Now, there were four schools, more than 6,000 students, and some new challenges.
Hansell had journeyed a lifetime for this opportunity. He thought about enduring the rigors of his double master's degrees at Montevallo, the specialist degree at Jacksonville State, and the bumps along the road of experience which all led him to this pinnacle in his profession. Hansell took over the district without any hesitation or reservations and worked the next three years to make difference. His achievements resulted in his being recognized as the Citizen of the Year by

the Okolona Chamber of Commerce. Hansell closed his tenure as Superintendent with a balanced budget and improved test scores.

Chapter 34
Ascending to the Top

Dr. Lonnie J. Edwards, Sr.

In 2008, Lonnie was tapped for an opportunity to return home to his birth state. Out of twenty-one (21) candidates, he was selected as the Superintendent of Jackson Public Schools (JPS) in Jackson, Mississippi – the capital city.

Accepting this position, Lonnie took on perhaps his greatest career challenge. The district had failing schools, poor test scores, racial issues, and funding challenges, and in much need for leader who was a capable change agent.
Clearly, Lonnie was born for this moment.

Lonnie's years of toiling behind the scenes in DeKalb Schools, working with race relations in White Plains, New York, as well as his employment with the Georgia Department of Education had prepared him for this position. He was honored to have the opportunity to serve the Jackson community of 136,000 people, with a student population of 32,000. The hands that once picked cotton in Mississippi fields were now picking people and securing resources as the leader of the state's largest school district.

After taking the helm of JPS, Lonnie hit the ground running, performing a needs assessment of the district. After reviewing the results, he busied himself daily meeting those needs. Doing so, he established an exemplary shared leadership style that made him a success wherever he went, in spite of encountering obstacles along the journey.

Over the next three years, between 2008-2011, Lonnie and his team laid a solid foundation on which future leaders could build. Under his leadership, they ...

- Collaboratively developed and managed a budget of $500,000,000 which supported the operations of a school district with 30,000+ students, 5,000 employees, and 63 schools
- Managed a $150,000,000 Capital Improvement Program which included building five (5) new schools; five (5) new athletic field houses; and major expansions or renovations schools
- Presented a balanced budget to the Board each year during tenure with no layoffs
- Instituted an on-going assessment process for students and teachers to determine needs and to provide support to ensure progress and developmental success
- Observed, achieved, and validated measurable improvements in student achievement according to state and federal assessment guidelines, had no schools ranked as "Failing"
- Established the Summer Leadership Institute for all administrators
- Established a partnership with an internationally renowned athlete which resulted in a donation of approximately $500,000 worth of exercise equipment to the district
- Established a partnership with Transformation Jackson, a faith-based organization, which resulted in approximately $2,000,000 worth of contributions

- Established partnerships with local faith-based leaders to support education initiatives
- Hosted First Lady Michelle Obama as she kicked-off her "Let's Move" wellness initiative in the district
- And more!

Jackson City Council President
Frank Bluntson, Ward 4

219 South President Street
Post Office Box 17
Jackson, Mississippi 39205-0017

Harvey Johnson, Jr.
Mayor of the City of Jackson

October 26, 2011

Dear Dr. Edwards,

Please find enclosed a small compilation of some of your accomplishments as superintendent of the Jackson Public School District. It is because of your hard work and dedication to the District that students and staff will continue to achieve greatness for years to come.

I am proud that I had an opportunity to work with you during your tenure as superintendent, and I sincerely appreciate your role in the District's success.

With best wishes,

Frank Bluntson

Jackson Public School District Reports on Student Academic Achievement For Year 2010 - 2011

Fourth-grade teachers at Bates Elementary School receive recognition for their outstanding work with children to become a High Performing School. (Bernisha Stamps, Gail Lewis, Cassandra Barrett, and Mitchell Shears)

Fifth-grade teachers at Bates Elementary School receive recognition for their outstanding work with come a High Performing School. (Connie May, Ebony Clark, Kimberly Archie, Wendy Smith and Mik

Schools recognized for student academic achievem

The Mississippi Link Newswire

Twenty-five JPS schools achieved successful or higher ratings in the state accountability results released in September by the Mississippi Department of Education. The schools were recognized during the Sept. 20 regular meeting of the JPS School Board. Interim Superintendent Dr. Jayne Sargent and the JPS School Board presented trophies and certificates to be displayed at each school.

The ratings are based on the results of state tests administered in spring 2011. The schools posting the most significant gains include:

• Davis Magnet Elementary, advancing from High Performing to Star

• Watkins Elementary, advancing two levels from Successful to Star

• Isabelleson Elementary, ad-

vancing two levels from Academic Watch to High Performing

• Chastain Middle School, advancing from Academic Watch to Successful

• Forest Hill High School, maintaining its Successful rating

Successful Schools - Baker Elem., Dr. Shauna Nicholson-Johnson, principal; John Hopkins

Elem., Dr. Nehru Brown, principal; Johnson Elem., Faith Strong, principal; Key Elem., Elaine Woods, principal; Lake Elem., Althea Johnson, principal; Pecan Park Elem.,

Wanda Quon, principal; Smith Elem., Dr. Mathis Sheriff, principal; Spann Elementary, Nicole Meneefi, principal; Walton Elem., Dr. Gwendolyn Gardner, principal;

pal; Forest Hill I Middle, Dr. Vinson and Van Winkle E Walker-Brown, pr

High Performing Schools - Bates Elem., Mitchell Shears, principal; Green Elem., Yavonka McGee, principal; Timberlawn Elem., Dr. Tennette Smith, principal; Barr Elem., Candra Nelson, principal; Bradley Elem., Dionne Woody, principal; Casey Elem., Leslie Coleman, principal; French Elem., Sebrona Brown, principal; and McLeod Elem., Dr. Courtney Sheriff, principal

Star Schools - McWillie Elem., Dr. Margrit Wallace, principal; Watkins Elem. Johnson, principal; George Elem., Mary Ann Bailey, principal; Power APAC Martin, principal; and Davis Magnet Elem., Dr. Jayne Everly, principal

THE WHITE House

March 30, 2010

Dr. Lonnie J. Edwards Superintendent
Jackson Public Schools
Post Office Box 2338
Jackson, Mississippi 39225-2338

Dear Lonnie:

Thank you so much for helping with my visit to Mississippi. I know how much hard work goes into an event like this, and I appreciate all of the time and energy you put in to make the event such a success.

I am so grateful to have had the opportunity to work with you on this important issue. Childhood obesity is a challenge that we must face together as one Nation, and I am inspired by the work being done to help realize the promise of a brighter, healthier tomorrow for our children. We can solve this problem only with the continued dedication of people like you.

Thank you again for the hard work that made this event possible, and for all of your hard work every day. I wish you all the best.

Sincerely,

Michelle Obama

Michelle Obama

(L-R) Dr. Lonnie J. Edwards, Sr., First Lady Michelle Obama, Mrs. Cynthia Dorsey Edwards

(L-R) First Lady Michelle Obama and Dr. Edwards at meeting in Mississippi to kick-off her "Let's Move" initiative in the Jackson Public School District to combat childhood obesity

Chapter 35
Finally, In Charge HIS Way

Hansell's experience "in the system" made him weary of politics but did not stymie his passion for finding more effective ways of helping educate children. He never forgot the little boy (himself) standing in class at the blackboard, counting on his fingers and being laughed at by his classmates. Upon his return to Alabama where he got his teaching start, Hansell kept busy biding his time with substitute teaching and eventually working as a principal at Midfield High School. What was clear to him was that he had become disillusioned with the quality of education in our public schools and that he needed to do something about it.

Gunn Christian Academy
Est. 2013

Therefore, in 2013, Hansell made a quantum leap of faith and opened his own school, Gunn Christian Academy. Doing this had been a desire most of his adult life.

So, after 39 years in the public sector, Hansell began life anew as Chancellor/Director/Owner of a small Christian academy.

During its operations, it served at-risk students, grades one through twelve. Its student body was ninety-nine percent black and one percent white, mostly from low socioeconomic backgrounds and living in challenging neighborhoods and surroundings. The Academy had a diverse staff of twelve teachers, and its classroom size averaged 10-12 students. Gunn Christian Academy held classes four days a week, Monday through Thursday. The sports teams received recognition and several awards in Football, Basketball and Golf.

GCA Cross-country team

Champion Golf

Track Team

The Academy also offered an Independent Adult Studies Program for the mature student, age 19 and older. Prior to 2014, the State of Alabama required a student to take a graduation examination prior to receiving a diploma. If the student did not pass the four areas of testing, they did not graduate even if they were successful in all areas of study in the classroom. Hansell was amazed at the number of people who had not graduated! Of course, there was a whole group of others who, for other reasons, were high school dropouts. This program allowed many students to get their long delayed High School Diplomas. After graduating, some students applied for and received promotions on their jobs, others were afforded the opportunity to get a job, some went on to college or Tech School. Finally, there were those who "just" wanted a high school diploma. The Academy closed in 2020 after seven wonderful years of operation.

L-R Hansell Gunn, former owner of The Gunn Christian Academy; Robert R. Reilly, former Alabama Governor; Dr. Levan Parker, former owner of Central Park Christian Academy in Birmingham; Del Marsh, Alabama State Senator

This once shy, quiet boy from Una, Mississippi is no longer being laughed at and is no longer afraid. His time at Montevallo opened his insolated and isolated world. This Silent Integrator has become a respected educational leader and a former chancellor of his own school where he continued to make a difference as a change agent.

Chapter 36
"Retired," But Still Leading and Serving

Lonnie's time in Mississippi's largest school district was well spent as he left the district in better shape than he had found it --- on solid, sound footing with a balanced budget and an enthusiastic community of learners and leaders.

On the eve of closing his superintendency in Jackson, Mississippi, in his home state, Lonnie reflected on his past accomplishments, his life as an educator and athlete, the many lives he touched, and those who touched and shaped his life as well. It was through his love of sports and for people that he was able to carve out a career that would long outlast his days of dribbling and shooting a basketball. Sports would lead him from, through, and out of the cotton fields in Mississippi to become a four-time Collegiate Hall of Famer in both Mississippi and Alabama, into the world of academics, and launch him into a stellar career.

Stone Mountain team representing Georgia in the Senior Olympics
Top Row (L-R) Bobby Lawrence, Travis Grant, Kenneth Mayfield
Bottom Row (L-R) Jimmy Stubbs, Lonnie Edwards Sr., Robert Pritchett

Sports would also remain an important part of his life, keeping him with a focus on his personal health and wellness as well as encouraging his children and grandchildren to participate and excel in sports. He was a member of a basketball team in the Senior Olympics, representing the state of Georgia that won all of their games and were awarded the Gold Medal for their performance.

Stone Mountain Mountaineers receiving their Gold Medals in the Senior Olympics

In academics, a foundation was laid that would spur him to earn six college degrees, culminating in a doctorate, and give him the confidence and the knowledge he needed to lead. It was his time at the University of Montevallo that gave him the courage, tenacity, and wisdom to navigate the troubled waters of human relations, receiving numerous awards for his efforts, all while becoming a community service ambassador and advocate for all. Lonnie has maintained an active connection with the university over the years.

In 1992, he was inducted into the University of Montevallo's Sports Hall of Fame. During his acceptance speech, he revealed that, as an undergraduate, he had pulled his dorm's fire alarm in the middle of the night, sending fellow students out into the cold in retribution to the many "pranks" to which he and Hansell were subjected by some of them. After hearing this confession, Dean Wilkinson's response was, "You rascal!" with a hearty laugh!

Since then, he has served on the UM Foundation Board and has received the following honors from the University of Montevallo:

- Invited to be the Keynote Speaker at Founder's Day 2019

- Presented the President's Award as a Distinguished Alumnus & Educator, 2019

- The Distinguished Minority Alumnus Award, Minority Alumni Association, 2017

- The establishment of the Dr. Lonnie J. Edwards, Sr. Award, presented annually to an Outstanding Minority Alumnus, by the UM Minority Alumni Association, 2017

This photo includes Dr. Frank and Dr. Bobbye Lightfoot (L-R: seats 2 and 3 on front row) next to Dr. Lonnie J. Edwards Sr.; Second row standing above Dr. Edwards is Mrs. Cynthia Dorsey Edwards

After leaving Jackson, MS, Lonnie returned home to Georgia and has remained active in developing educational projects as well as in local government.

Through Edwards & Associates, Inc., Lonnie is focusing on two key audiences: young children and the adult learner. As representatives of the Tools For Life® Program, an evidenced-based resource that influences positive child development and leads to better futures, Lonnie and his team trained educators and parents on social emotional learning (SEL) skills. This program is designed to aid early learning centers and schools, through the eighth grade, in improving behavioral and relationship-building skills of students. Social emotional learning skills are credited with helping to improve academic performance and to reduce the extraordinary number of students disciplined, suspended, or expelled for inappropriate behaviors, even in pre-school!

Lonnie is also passionate about assisting and supporting

individuals who did not complete high school as lacking this basic educational credential limits one's military and employment options as well as one's resulting quality of life. Prior to his retirement from the DeKalb County School District, Lonnie initiated a successful dropout recovery program. Adults who had dropped out of school and who wanted to earn a high diploma and get help with job placement were recruited. The event was held on a Saturday and attracted huge crowds seeking help. Many attendees were connected with the school system or with local colleges to earn their high school diplomas or GEDs. Lonnie is still advocating for this population in many settings and connecting those who need this assistance to proper resources.

Edwards & Associates website: www.educationbeyondboundaries.com

Receiving the Community Service Award from WXIA-TV, Channel 11, Atlanta, GA
(L-R) Brenda Woods, WXIA Anchor; Dr. Edwards and wife, Cynthia Dorsey Edwards

In 2021, Lonnie was selected by Georgia state legislators as one of 9 people, including 2 alternates, to serve on the DeKalb County Board of Ethics for a term of three years. By law, the Ethics Board is completely independent of the DeKalb CEO, Commissioners, and any officers or employees of DeKalb County government. Board members serve on a volunteer basis and their role is as follows:

- To provide Advisory Opinions to all officials and employees who seek advice on ethical issues
- To receive and hear complaints regarding ethical violations of employees and officials in DeKalb
- To investigate matters brought by third parties or the Ethics Officer regarding potential violations of the Ethics Code
- To establish Rules regarding its matters within its jurisdiction and provide forms for disclosure

At the first meeting of the Board seated in 2021, Lonnie was voted by other Board members to serve as its chairman. This Silent Integrator from Mississippi, Alabama, and Georgia continues to be engaged in activities which embrace the ideals of fairness and ethical behavior.

In recognition of his being a pioneer in helping to integrate the University of Montevallo, Lonnie was featured in an interview on a local news station in Birmingham, Alabama, Channel CBS 42, in a story title, "Hidden History."
Video - https://youtu.be/AYhV9gGao_0

From his young adult life, Lonnie supported fair, equitable, and equal rights for all. Sometimes, he was actively involved; sometimes, he was vocal; and sometimes, he appeared silent, quietly working behind the scenes with others to facilitate change.

As previously shared, besides Biblical verses guiding his life, Lonnie also internalized the words of Robert Frost's poem and included them among his leading principles.

The Road Not Taken

Two roads diverged in a yellow wood,
And sorry I could not travel both
And be one traveler, long I stood
And looked down one as far as I could
To where it bent in the undergrowth;

Then took the other, as just as fair,
And having perhaps the better claim,
Because it was grassy and wanted wear;
Though as for that the passing there
Had worn them really about the same,

And both that morning equally lay
In leaves no step had trodden black.
Oh, I kept the first for another day!
Yet knowing how way leads on to way,
I doubted if I should ever come back.

I shall be telling this with a sigh
Somewhere ages and ages hence:
Two roads diverged in a wood, and I—
I took the one less traveled by,
And that has made all the difference.

Robert Frost - 1874-1963

EPILOGUE

Both Lonnie and Hansell have become known as change agents and transformational leaders, all with the good of others in mind. What an accomplishment and legacy to leave for one's time here on this earth!

There are several thoughts that Lonnie and Hansell would like for the reader to take from their journey:

1. Recognize and give honor to God ... or to your higher power ... and continuously thank them for your blessings; ask them for guidance and direction in your life and in your decision-making.
2. Non-violent means can be used effectively to make significant changes.
3. You cannot judge a book by its cover. Remember that your greatest allies may not look like you but may have your best interest at heart.
4. When you are blessed, reach back, over, up, and down to help and bless others.
5. Don't always look to others to solve problems, many times the solutions are within your own capabilities.
6. Don't hesitate to ask for help when needed --- before a disaster strikes.
7. Don't be afraid. Step out of your comfort zone. Take calculated risks.
8. Show appreciation to individuals in your support system. Don't take people and their kindness to you for granted.
9. Respect yourself and others. Your behavior teaches others how to treat you.
10. Remember that keeping a positive focus on human relations will help to address race relations.
11. Learn, understand, use, and share principles of social emotional learning. They will help in all challenges in life - for children and adults - in the classroom, in the home, in businesses, and in our community at-large.
12. Always consider traveling the road less taken. It could make all the difference in your life

After taking the journey with Lonnie and Hansell, transitioning from segregation to integration and having an understanding of some of the impacts they have made and are still making on our world, I leave you with this question, "What legacy are you leaving?"

Appendix A

Still Connected with the University of Montevallo

Lonnie and Hansell have remained engaged with and have become active supporters of the University of Montevallo (UM). In 2022, they visited the college and participated in a discussion reflecting on the changes from segregation to integration to today's environment. Calvin Cylk Cozart, actor, director, producer, and writer facilitated this discussion.

Shown in the photo with Cylk, Lonnie, and Hansell are UM current and former administrators (L-R) Dr. John W. Stewart, III, 15th President of UM; Dr. Leon Davis, former Director of Athletics; and the current Director of Athletics, Mark Richard.

Dr. Davis and Dr. Edwards share a serious moment of reflections on the past.

Lonnie & Hansell share a moment of laughter with Dr. Davis in-between games.

(L-R) Hansell Gunn, Jr., Dr. Leon Davis, and Dr. Lonnie Edwards

(L-R) Hansell Gunn, Jr., Mark Richard, and Dr. Lonnie Edwards

Dr. Lonnie Edwards and Dr. Jeanette Crew, UM Professor (taught square dancing)

University of Montevallo Foundation Board of Directors

Black Alumni Club, University of Montevallo

The Legacy Continues! Lia Edwards, UM Freshman Class of 2023, Granddaughter of Dr. Lonnie J. Edwards, Sr. and Mrs. Cynthia Dorsey Edwards

Appendix B

Lonnie Johnson Edwards Sr., Ed. D.

JPS School Board selects new school head

By Gail M. Brown
Editor

The Board of Trustees of the Jackson Public Schools has selected Dr. Lonnie J. Edwards, Education Program specialist with the Georgia Department of Education, to serve as the district's next superintendent.

"Dr. Edwards's experience at the state level, coupled with his district-level work in the 100,000-student DeKalb County School System for 33 years, convinced a majority of the board that he is the right person for the job of superintendent at this time in Jackson's history," said School Board President Delmer Stamps.

Stamps said board members weighed the individual merits of each candidate, the sentiments of the various stakeholders, and the board's own scrutiny of the candidates' attributes and credentials before voting.

In addition to the comprehensive screening of the candidates' backgrounds, board members met with key education and community leaders in the two out-of-state candidates' hometowns to gain insight about the candidates' reputations. In the end, Dr. Edwards was approved by a 3-2 vote of the board.

"Dr. Edwards has impressive credentials and a reputation as a highly energetic and enthusiastic education leader in his community," said Stamps. "He is well known for thinking outside of the box and for getting things done in innovative ways. We need that."

Edwards, of Atlanta, served in various roles as an administrator for the DeKalb County School System: assistant superintendent for Business Affairs, assistant superintendent for

Edwards

Parental Involvement, Community & Support Programs; area assistant superintendent for Instruction and Administration, where he managed the administration and operations for elementary (including theme and magnet), middle, and high schools; and assistant superintendent for Elementary Administration, where he managed the administrative operations for 84 elementary principals, 175 assistant principals, 5,000 faculty, and 55,000 students.

His district level experience in the DeKalb

New Superintendent
Continued on page 2

Superintendent, Jackson Public Schools, Jackson, Mississippi 2008-2011

Lonnie Johnson Edwards Sr., Ed. D.

Dr. Lonnie J. Edwards Sr. is the President/CEO of Edwards & Associates, Inc., an educational consulting firm. He has served as a senior executive in the field of Education and is a knowledgeable educator, an effective workshop presenter, and a highly sought-after motivational speaker.

Dr. Edwards' diverse, senior-level leadership experience enables him to work effectively with clients to identify major challenges/roadblocks in meeting their organizational goals as well as to find, select, and implement resources/solutions to address them. He is experienced in and passionate about strategies that focus on social and emotional learning, parental involvement, drop-out recovery and re-engagement, school redesign, community/stakeholder relations, and professional and leadership development. He has a vast network of professionals on which he can draw to meet the needs of Edwards & Associates' clients.

Dr. Edwards earned a Doctorate in School Administration and Management from Atlanta University (now Clark Atlanta University) in Atlanta, GA. His dissertation thesis was "A Study to Assess the Factors Which Impact the Long-Range Teacher Potential Pool Among High School Seniors in the DeKalb County School System." His doctoral program included international study at the University of West Indies in Mona, Jamaica. Dr. Edwards earned two master's degrees in School Administration and Physical Education from the University of Montevallo, Montevallo, AL; a bachelor's degree in Physical Education and Psychology at Montevallo University; & an associate degree from Coahoma Junior College, Clarksdale, MS.

Born and reared on his family's farm in rural Mississippi, Dr. Edwards was successful in maneuvering from Coahoma Junior College, a two-year, predominately Black college to Montevallo University, a predominately White college, where he was the first African American male athlete recruited and admitted to the school. Dr. Edwards graduated with honors and was inducted into the Basketball Hall of Fame at both institutions.

After his professional basketball career ended prematurely, Dr. Edwards was employed by the DeKalb School System, located east of Atlanta, GA and one of the largest public educational systems in the state (100,000+ students), from 1971 until his retirement in 2004. During that time, he progressively moved up "the career ladder" from teacher to Assistant Superintendent. In 2005, Edwards & Associates was engaged by the White Plains School District, in White Plains, NY, to assist them in diversity management. In 2006, Dr. Edwards resumed full-time employment with the Georgia Department of Education as an Education Program Specialist for Federal Programs.

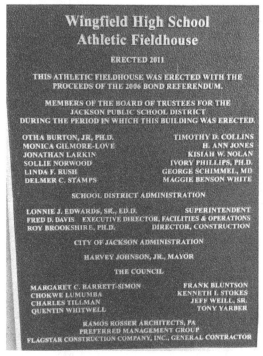

This plaque is one placed in schools and athletic field houses to acknowledge major school renovations as well as those instrumental in ensuring that they are completed.

From 2008-2011, Dr. Edwards served as the Superintendent of the Jackson Public School District in Jackson, Mississippi, with a staff of more than 5,000 employees; a student enrollment of 30,600; 63 schools; and a budget in excess of $500,000,000. He managed a $150,000,000 Capital Improvement Program which included building five (5) new schools; five (5) new athletic field houses; and making major expansions or renovations to existing schools. As a result of Dr. Edwards' time in Jackson, measurable improvements in student achievement were observed, achieved, and validated.

In 1996, Dr. Edwards was featured on the *Sally Jessy Raphael Show* for making a significant difference in the life of a former student who was born with a physical disability. As a result of his impact on this student's life, Dr. Edwards authored a book entitled, **A Teacher's Touch: Reaching Beyond Boundaries** and established a foundation to provide college scholarships for students with disabilities.

For his service to the community, Dr. Edwards has received many awards and recognitions, including Atlanta's **WXIA-TV 11-Alive's Community Service Award**. In 2020, the Dr. Martin Luther King Jr. Advisory Council for the State of Georgia presented him with its **first award in the field of Education**. In 2019, he received the **President's Award as a Distinguished Alumnus & Educator** from the University of Montevallo, Montevallo, AL and was also an inductee in the Clarksdale/Coahoma County, **Mississippi Sports Hall of Fame**. Also, in 2019 and 2020, he served as a guest speaker for the Humphrey Fellowship Program, based at the Rollins School of Public Health, Emory University. In 2017, the Minority Alumni Association at the University of Montevallo established the **Dr. Lonnie J. Edwards, Sr. Outstanding Minority Alumnus Award** and presented the first award to him. In 2007, Dr. Edwards was inducted into the **Mississippi Community & Junior College Sports Hall of Fame** as one of its 45 charter members. He was selected to receive this honor for his noteworthy contributions on and off the basketball court. In 2003, he was selected as Coahoma Community College's **"Top Role Model"** for an educational ad campaign which was publicized throughout the state of Mississippi. Also, in 2003, he was selected to be a member of the Board of Directors for the **Georgia Partnership for Excellence in Education** for the 2003-2004 term.

A few other awards presented to Dr. Edwards include: **Congressional Black Caucus, Education Technology Think Tank Braintrust, Champion Award**; **Certificate of Special Congressional Recognition**, presented by

Congressman John Lewis; **Jefferson Award for Public Service** from the American Institute for Public Service, Washington, D.C.; **Key to the City of Selma, AL**, at the City-wide Celebration for Dr. Martin Luther King's Birthday; Georgia Legislative Black Caucus, **Excellence in Education Award**; **Proclamation, signed by Governor Zell Miller, State of Georgia**; and the **NAIA Service Master Distinguished Graduate Award**. He was also a member of the **2001 Men's National Basketball Team Gold Medal Winners in the Senior Olympics Games**.

Dr. Edwards is married to Cynthia Dorsey Edwards who retired as a Vice President at Georgia Piedmont Technical College in Clarkston, GA. They have three adult children and six grandchildren.

ACHIEVEMENTS & HONORS

- First award in the field of Education by the Dr. Martin Luther King Jr. Advisory Council for the State of Georgia, 2020
- President's Award as a Distinguished Alumnus & Educator, the University of Montevallo, Montevallo, AL, 2019
- Inductee, Clarksdale/Coahoma County, Mississippi Sports Hall of Fame, 2019
- Guest speaker for the Humphrey Fellowship Program, the Rollins School of Public Health, Emory University, 2019/20
- Selected as the Distinguished Minority Alumnus, Minority Alumni Association, University of Montevallo, 2017
- Honored with the establishment of the Dr. Lonnie J. Edwards Award, to be awarded annually to an Outstanding Minority Alumnus, by the Minority Alumni Association, University of Montevallo, 2017
- Keynote Speaker at the City-wide Dr. King Celebration; Presented the Key to the City of Clarksdale, MS, 2017
- Dr. Martin Luther King Jr. Man of the Year Award, Jackson, MS, 2010
- Image Award in the Field of Education, Phi Beta Sigma Fraternity, Jackson, MS, 2010
- Inductee, Mississippi Community & Junior College/Sports Hall of Fame, Charter Member, 2007
- Congressional Black Caucus, Education Technology Think Tank Braintrust, Champion Award, 2004
- Coahoma Community College's "Top Role Model" – Education Ad Campaign in Mississippi, 2003
- Georgia Partnership for Excellence in Education, Board Member, 2003-2004
- Certificate of Special Congressional Recognition, presented by Congressman John Lewis, 2003

- All Children Are Special – Champion Award for Educational Empowerment, 2003
- Toney Gardens Civic Association, Outstanding Service Award, 2002
- Author of ***A Teacher's Touch: Reaching Beyond Boundaries***, published 2001
- WXIA-TV 11-Alive Community Service Award, Atlanta, GA, 2001
- Jefferson Award for Public Service from the American Institute for Public Service, Washington, D.C.,2001
- Member of the Men's (50+) National Basketball Team Gold Medal Winners in the Senior Olympics Games, 2001
- Presented a Key to the City of Selma, AL, at the City-wide Celebration for Dr. Martin Luther King's Birthday, 2001
- National Women of Achievement, Profiles in Prominence Award, 2001
- Georgia Legislative Black Caucus, Excellence in Education Award, 2000
- Proclamation, signed by Governor Zell Miller, State of Georgia, 1996
- DeKalb County Board of Education Recognition Award, 1996
- Appearance on the Sally Jessy Raphael Show for Making a Difference in a Student's Life, 1996
- Breakfast Club Annual Community Service Award, 1995
- Club Colombia Human Relations and Diversity, 1994
- NAIA Service Master Distinguished Graduate Award, 1993
- Inducted into the University of Montevallo's Sports Hall of Fame, 1992
- Native American Human Relations Award, 1990
- Educational Research Foundation for School Improvement Presentation, 1987
- DeKalb Branch of NAACP Education Award, 1985

- DeKalb Board of Education, Resolution for Outstanding Service to Community, 1985
- Inducted into Coahoma Junior College's Sports Hall of Fame, 1983
- Honorary Special Deputy Sheriff, DeKalb County, 1978
- Honorary Life Membership in the Georgia Congress of Parents and Teachers, 1973
- Invited as Participant to Atlanta Hawks Basketball Camp, 1972
- Invited as Participant to Chicago Bulls Rookie Camp, 1971
- Selected as an Outstanding College Athlete of America, 1971
- Circle K Sportsman Award University of Montevallo, 1971
- Basketball Team Captain, University of Montevallo, 1970-71
- Varsity Letters, Trophies and Awards in Basketball, 1969-71
- Selected to Who's Who in America Among Colleges and Universities, 1969

Appendix C

Hansell Gunn, Jr., Ed. S.

Okolona School District: A New Beginning
by Superintendent Hansell Gunn

The Okolona Municipal Separate School District began the 2006-2007 school year with a renewed commitment to excellence. The administration, faculty and staff are committed to providing an educational setting that is second to none for the students of this district.

As educational leaders, the administration will strive to promote the success of all students in this school district. In order to do this, the principals and the superintendent have made and will continue to make every effort to ensure that the school environment is one that is safe, efficient, and effective in order that each student will be able to achieve at his/her highest potential. This year the commitment began with a great improvement in the school's aesthetics. This summer the hallways of the Okolona Elementary School three story building received a facelift with a beautiful new paint job. The renovation - which separated junior high students from high school students is one that has long been needed. Research indicates that adolescence is a critical stage in learning; therefore, to accommodate these students, junior high students will be housed on a separate hall of the school. This year junior high students will have little interaction with high school students. This change will give junior high students the opportunity to achieve the necessary academic preparation and maturity needed for high school success. Although there are many changes being made this year, the mission of the Okolona School District remains same - to provide a safe and orderly environment where students have the opportunity to excel academically, artistically, technologically and athletically.

In the quest for academic excellence, the Okolona School District has added several new members to its staff: at the Okolona Elementary School: Johnie Franks, kindergarten; Mandy Hunt, kindergarten; Sheryl Denton,

Bridgett Edwards, facilitator for the electronic classroom and the career; and Kela Glenn and Ruby Buchanan, special education.

Not only has the district added new personnel, but both Okolona High School and Okolona Elementary School are upgrading the curriculum. Okolona High School has added a new course, pre-algebra, to the seventh grade curriculum. Those students who do well on assessment in the pre-algebra class will be assigned algebra I when they enter the eigth grade. Also, there are smaller class sizes in the core subjects (mathematics, English, science and social studies). This provides the teacher with more time for individualized instruction. For the first time this year, Okolona High School will offer three classes of Spanish I. Using the SPMS (Student Progress Monitoring System), both Okolona High School and Okolona Elementary School will track student progress. This program will allow teachers to assess the strengths and weaknesses of individual students, plan individualized instruction, and provide on-going pertinent academic information to parents.

In continuing to provide academically for the students of the Okolona School District, Okolona Elementary School received the Reading First Grant for the third year. This grant supplies teachers with materials to remediate and assess the students' strengths and weaknesses in reading. The students are given a reading assessment three times per year, which is called the Dynamic Indicators of Basic Early Literacy Skills (DIBELS). The test measures Letter Naming Fluency (LNF), and Phoneme Segmentation Fluency (PSF). There were sixty-three schools that participated in Reading First last school term; Okolona Elementary School ranked number 21 in growth in LNF, 29 in PSF, and 1 in ORF.

Many improvements have also been made in the areas of art and athletics. Both the general music and art classes have grown. General music and art are being offered to all junior high school students. The Chieftain Pride Band has grown from twenty-two members in 2005-2006 to seventy members for this school year. The number of players on the football team has increased, and the OHS cheerleaders will be in new uniforms this year.

The many changes that are being made this year are in keeping with the mission of the Okolona School District to provide a safe and orderly environment where the students have the opportunity to excel academically, artistically, technologically, and athletically.

Hansell Gunn, Jr., Ed. S.

Hansell Gunn, Jr. was born in Mississippi, the oldest of three children. He attended public schools in the city of the West Point, MS. After high school, he completed an AA degree at Coahoma Junior College in Coahoma MS. He was all set to finish his two remaining years at Jackson State University; those plans were set aside when he left the state to complete his historical undergraduate degree at the University of Montevallo. He and a fellow Coahoman were the first two African American student-athletes to graduate from the University. While those were turbulent times in the history of the United States of America, they successfully completed their B.S. degrees. These two were the first African American students to play basketball at the university. Mr. Gunn went on to desegregate the school's baseball team. He deliberately chose the number 42 (the number worn by Jackie Robinson), as his jersey number. Mr. Gunn excelled in his academic studies and in sports, earning athletic scholarships to attend both Colleges.

His first position was middle school teacher and coach (baseball, football, and basketball), at Vestavia Junior High School in Vestavia, Alabama. All teams received various honors in his two- year tenure. While working at Vestavia, the completed his master's degree at the University of Montevallo.

The former Glenn High School of Birmingham was the next stop for Mr. Gunn. He worked as teacher and coached basketball. His first year at the school, his team was undefeated and winners of the Alabama State Basketball Tournament. He coached the first female varsity basketball player in the state during this tenure, returning to the state to compete in the Tournament. While the team was not number one in the tournament, they were number one in the news and in the hearts of young girls all over the state seeking equality in high school sports.

Mr. Gunn then turned his attention to Education Administration in Georgia. He served as Assistant Principal at

Peachtree Jr. High school in North DeKalb County. After two years, the then Governor of the state recommended him for the position of Principal at Douglas Middle School in Thomasville, GA. How does one refuse a recommendation from the governor, right? He had much success at mending the very broken fences between not only the community but between the Black and White citizens of the community.

After four years, he returned to North Fulton County, GA to work again at Peachtree Junior High school. During this tenancy, he obtained his Education Specialist degree from Jacksonville State University, Alabama. This degree positioned him for the position of Principal at Banneker High School in that same county.

He had remarkable success at Banneker High School, going from "worst" to "first" in the state ranking of schools and earning "The Blue-Ribbon School" award. This prestigious honor is awarded to an elementary, middle, and high school in each state, each year. Mr. Gunn brought many programs to the school; included were mentorships, community involvement, and corporate engagement. Members of the Atlanta Braves, Falcons, and Hawks offered services in their respective sports teams. Several national magazines acknowledged the school with awards and accolades for the leadership supplied and the improvements made in mending the existing fences between the school and the community as well as in improving and increasing parental involvement. The "Hip Hop Music" influence was new and growing at that time; the high school produced several talented students who became members of a couple of billboards "Hip Hop" groups. Mr. Gunn received the Superintendent's award two straight years while employed in Fulton County, GA.

Ready for a new challenge, Mr. Gunn moved to Colorado. He worked as Assistant Principal at two different middle schools in the state, (Wheatridge and West) before returning to the more challenging position as Montebello High School principal. This school benefited from the experience attained at the "Blue Ribbon School." Some of the same strategies were implemented to build the fences between the school, the community, and corporate America. Although the school did not reach the country's top honor, Mr. Gunn received countless state and community awards and acknowledgements.

Heeding the call to return South to aid in the care of aging parents and parents-in-law, Mr. Gunn returned to his hometown as Principal of the school from which he graduated - Fifth Street Junior High. It was then a high school. One of his greatest accomplishments during the year he was there was the removal of an ugly chain-linked fence topped with barbed wire that surrounded the campus. He likened it to the wire fences used to surround prisons. A beautiful black wrought iron fence replaced it and now enhances and complements the school as well as the community.

Mr. Gunn's final tenancy, or so he thought, was spent as Superintendent of a school system just north of his birth city, Okolona Municipal District. Although, his plan was to retire after he left Okolona, he worked one more year in Mississippi, at Aberdeen High School; one with a first- year principal. Delaying retirement one more year, he worked as the Assistant Principal and Athletic Director.

Moving to Alabama, a strategic location between his parents and parents-in-law, he thought he would do volunteer work the rest of his days with freedom to take care of his parents as needed. He did volunteer work here and there, but the calling on his life gave him no peace. He loves children and has a heart for "at-risk" children and their education access. His motto has always been "You must reach them to teach them."

He started working as substitute teacher but soon began work as principal at Midfield High School. He experienced such displeasure at the "system's" way of educating that he decided to pursue opening his own school. This had been a desire most of his adult life. So, after 39 years in the public sector, he began life anew as Chancellor/Director/Owner of a small Christian Academy. When the opportunity presented itself,

Gunn Christian Academy became a reality!

Founded in 2013, the Academy closed in 2020 after seven wonderful years of operation. The Academy also offered a successful Independent Adult Studies Program designed for the "mature" student. Retirement was perhaps the only thing he did not do well!

Mr. Gunn is married to the former Wilda Y. Vines. They are parents of Leslie Michelle Gunn and Jonathan Michael Gunn.

HANSELL GUNN, JR., ED. S.

ACHIEVEMENTS AND HONORS
- Who's Who in American Junior Colleges
- Outstanding Young Men of America Award
- Outstanding Student Athlete, University of Montevallo
- Honors Graduate, University of Montevallo
- College Athlete of America Award
- 3A Coach of the Year
- Certificate of Appreciation – Guest Speaker 8th Annual DLCI Scholarship Banquet
- Community Service and Support Award – Bennie Hill Goodwin Educational Foundation

- ## Fulton County (Atlanta Georgia)
- Fulton County, GA Superintendent's Award (2 years)
- Georgia Educational Leadership Academy Certification of Merit
- Principal – 5th District Secondary School of Excellence
- Selected by the State of Georgia to access quality of Secondary Education
- Principal – Redbook Magazine America's Best School
- Citizen of the Year Award
- Certificate of Appreciation, guest speaker, Great Park Hill Sertoma Club

- ## Okolona MS School District
- Implementation of District-wide Uniform Policy (98% support from parents, students, community) -Okolona MS School District
- Implemented the District's first Academic Award Achievement Ceremony
- Increased graduation rate by 10%
- Reduced Dropout rate from 49% to 17% in 2 years
- Raised District achievement rating from level 2 to level 3 in 2 years
- All Schools made AYP (Average Yearly Progress)

- Implemented Parent Volunteer/Community Involvement Program
- Saturday School to Improve Academic Improvement
- Induction into the Montevallo University Hall of Fame
- Founder/Chancellor Gunn Christian Academy
- Expanding the Vision, Aurora CO, Co-Ordinator

In Memoriam

Coach Bill Jones

1936 – 2008

Bill Jones was a decorated athlete and coach, a loving husband and a devoted father and grandfather who brought a smile to everyone he encountered. He was born May 12, 1936, in Lauderdale County. After graduating from Lexington High School, he earned a basketball scholarship to Florence State College, now the University of North Alabama. A successful collegiate athletic career encouraged him to follow his passion into coaching. His dedication, focus, and his complete understanding of the game of basketball led him to success at Lauderdale County High School, Opelika High School, Marion Military Institute, and the University of Montevallo. Coach Jones recruited and provided scholarships

for Lonnie and Hansell to become the first African American male student-athletes at the University of Montevallo. He was inducted posthumously as a member of the Alabama Sports Hall of Fame Class of 2013 for his success at the University of North Alabama as a player, coach, and Athletic Director.

Wilburn Mike Adams

1924 – 2009

A signalman aboard the Destroyer Escort Eugene E. Elmore in World War II. A life-long athlete and winner of the Boston Marathon for the over-60 age group. A devoted husband who stood by his wife as she faced Alzheimer's disease. A generous and loving father and grandfather. Wilburn Adams was all of these things during a full and faithful 85 years that ended peacefully on the morning of July 17, 2009.

Mr. Adams was an aggressive proponent of the integration of public schools in Selma, Alabama and DeKalb County, Georgia. As Associate Superintendent of both Selma and DeKalb County Schools, he spent his career quietly, yet effectively, working on behalf of positive change and equal opportunity for students with disabilities and for people of all races. His colleagues, friends, and family describe him as a man of honor and character who never stopped giving and teaching. Mr. Adams was the first person that talked with Lonnie Edwards about employment as an Educator with the DeKalb County School System. Once he was hired, Mr. Adams was one of Dr. Edwards's most avid supporters and advocates.

Nancy B. Johnson

1959 - 2022

An unforgettable student!

The small voice with the loudest "Thank You" heard around the world was silenced April 1, 2022. Nancy B. Johnson, Texas native, Florida resident, and former student of the DeKalb County School District was a mother of 3 and grandmother of two. Born with vestiges of fingers, she hid her hands with a handkerchief every day when attending school to avoid ridicule from classmates. It was through her interaction with her gym teacher, Lonnie Edwards, that she gained the confidence to uncover her hands, play the piano, learn to type 65 words per minute, complete a bachelor's degree, secure and maintain jobs, and later raise a family.

DeKalb County, GA mourned the little girl from Hooper Alexander Elementary School who changed the course of human relations in the school district by simply saying "Thank You for Changing My Life!" to Dr. Edwards on the Sally Jessy Raphael Show in 1996.

To Nancy Johnson, we say "Thank You!" for valuing and highlighting what teachers do!

CPSIA information can be obtained
at www.ICGtesting.com
Printed in the USA
LVHW010522200723
752659LV00010B/167

9 798985 441123